Con

Conures as Pets

Conures book for care, costs, health, feeding, grooming and training.

By

Jodi Chapman

ALL RIGHTS RESERVED. This book contains material protected under International and Federal Copyright Laws and Treaties.

Any unauthorized reprint or use of this material is strictly prohibited. No part of this book may be reproduced or transmitted in any form or by any means, electronic, mechanical or otherwise, including photocopying or recording, or by any information storage and retrieval system without express written permission from the author.

Copyright © 2017

Published by: Zoodoo Publishing

Table of Contents

Introduction

Conures engage us from the first moment we catch sight of them: Their feathers are gorgeous, they seem to represent an exotic landscape, and they are as interested in us as we are in them. If you have not spent a lot of time with a conure, you may be surprised at the attention a conure gives to every detail of a human's movement and tone of voice.

And, in response, their attempts to get human attention are fascinating. The sounds they make, the way they move their bodies, the color of their feathers are interesting, but their fascination with us is gratifying—flattering even. Additionally, conures take us from the mundane, ordinary life of our homes and lead us to imagine life in a foreign and magical place.

Thanks for buying this book. It's my firm belief that it will provide you with all the answers to your questions

Below are the chapters tackled in this book:

A brief history of the conures
Here you will get a detailed discussion on the history of these small birds, how they were domesticated etc.

Why keep a conure
In this chapter, there are a number of reasons as to why conures are kept as pets.

All types of conures
Here you'll find information on many of the popular conure species. From the sun conure to the red throated conure, you've got a lot to choose from.

Choosing the right conure
This is where I start getting into the practicalities of sharing your home with a conure. You'll find all the information you need on proper conure housing and accessories.

Home sweet home
Bringing a conure home is an exciting day if you're prepared for it, and you'll find a lot of good information here that shows you how to conure-

proof your home, as well as where to place the cage and how to properly interact with your bird from day one.

Everyday care
In this chapter, you will get information on taking care of your conure.

Feeding your conure
Possibly the most important chapters are contained in this part. Conure nutrition is a controversial topic and certainly makes the difference between a healthy bird and a dead one. Hence, this is the most essential chapter in this entire book. After that, you'll find chapters on grooming and on health and illness.

Grooming your conure
Here you will get detailed information on grooming your conure to be super healthy and presentable.

Keeping your conure healthy
In this chapter, I'll list common normal parrot behaviors. Use them as a starting point to determine what behaviors are normal for your pet bird. Compare them against the list of abnormal behaviors, which can often indicate illness. Birds are experts at hiding signs of illness, so by the time a bird looks or acts sick, he is seriously ill.

Conure's behaviour
In this part, you'll find information on taming and training, and these may be the first chapters many people turn to when they get this book.

Having fun with your conure
Well, conure behavior isn't simple, but these chapters attempt to explain why conures do the funny and odd things that tend to baffle guardians.

You'll get information on both normal and abnormal companion bird behaviors, as well as advice for living in a multiple-conure household.

Chapter 1: A brief history of the Conures

Conures are New World parrots, which means they are native to the Americas. They were first found throughout Latin America, from Mexico through the islands of the Caribbean to southern Chile. The largest conure is the Patagonian conure, which is about seventeen and a half inches long, and the smallest is the painted conure, which is eight and a half inches long from the top of his head to the tip of his tail.

Conures' native environments include a wide variety of climates and terrains, from savannahs to tropical forests and cooler mountain areas. They are peaceful birds who live in large flocks. Conures' nesting sites in the wild range from niches carved into sandstone cliffs to tree cavities.

Some species, such as the red throat, olive throat, Cuban, and peach front, nest in active termite mounds or termite nests in trees. To do this, the birds break into the termite mound with their beaks and dig a tunnel and a nesting chamber. This effort takes them about a week, after which they leave the nest alone for a week so the termites can seal off the nest from the rest of the mound. The birds then return and set up housekeeping.

In the wild, conures eat a variety of foods, including grass seeds, fruits, cactus, berries, nuts, flowers, insects, and grains. They can also do damage to cultivated crops, which makes them unpopular with farmers in their native habitats.

The First Documented Conures

Conures were first described in literature in 1724 by Jean Baptiste Labat, a French priest who spent thirteen years as a missionary in the colonies of the West Indies. While there, he also studied and documented many of the native species of plants and animals he saw. Labat described and drew pictures of a species of bird he called Aratinga labati on the island of Guadaloupe. Some naturalists believe this green parrot with a few red head feathers may have been a captive Cuban conure (Aratinga euops), or he may now be an extinct species.

Conures began to be imported into Europe and the United States more than a hundred years ago, and a few species, such as the green conure, were being bred in the United States in the mid-1930s. Unfortunately, at the time most people believed it was easier to go into the jungle and capture wild birds, rather than setting up the birds they had in breeding colonies. With habitat destruction and the increased demand for birds in the pet trade, this situation had to change.

Domestic Breeding Begins
The brightly colored sun and jenday conures spurred aviculturists into breeding conures on a large scale. The sun conure was first imported into the United States in the 1960s, and these birds were routinely bred in captivity by the 1980s. The jenday conure soon followed.

After that, aviculturists turned their attention to other conure species, which turned out to be a benefit for both pet owners and wild conures. Pet owners received more suitable companion birds when domestic-bred conures were available, and wild conures were less threatened with trapping and exportation because the demand for them decreased.

Although wild-caught birds were still fairly common pets into the early 1980s, most conures offered for sale as pets are now domestically-bred birds. This means they are healthier and better suited emotionally to be petted than the wild-caught birds of twenty or twenty-five years ago.

Many Conure Species
Depending on which expert you consult, between forty-five and one hundred different species and subspecies of birds in six genera make up the group of parrots we call conures. This book does not include all of the different species because not all are commonly kept as pets.

This book focuses primarily on the Aratinga (pronounced ah-rah-ting-ah) and Pyrrhura (pronounced py-hurrah) genera, which include the most common pets. A few birds in other genera, such as Nandayus, Cyanoliseus, and Enicognathus, are discussed as well because they also make good pets.

One way to distinguish the two genera of conures is to remember that Aratinga birds are brightly colored (vibrant greens and reds, for example), while Pyrrhura birds are darker in coloration (deep green or maroon). Aratinga birds also lack the light-colored markings on the upper chest that Pyrrhura birds characteristically have.

Some breeders think conures and macaws are closely related. In fact, the genus name Aratinga means "little macaw." There are some physical similarities worth noting: similar body shapes, brightly colored feathers, and long tails. Further genetic analysis is needed to determine just how close the relationship is between these groups of birds.

Conure Characteristics

Conures are outgoing, cheerful, inquisitive little acrobats who take an active interest in their surroundings and the activities of their human family. They are also intelligent, playful, and extremely affectionate.

Although they are smaller members of the parrot family, conures have large personalities and sometimes seem to be unaware of or unable to remember their size.

Conures offer something for almost anyone. Some species are known to be cuddly, others can learn to talk fairly well, and still, others are strikingly beautiful. Most are also quite affordable pets.

Strange Sleeping Habits

Another interesting aspect of the conure personality is their tendency to snuggle under something when they sleep. Don't be surprised to find your bird under a corner of his cage paper if the cage he lives in doesn't have a grill to keep the bird out of the cage tray. You can provide your conure with a washcloth, a fuzzy toy, or something else cuddly to snuggle with.

Don't become alarmed the first time you see your conure asleep with his head tucked under his wing and resting on one leg. Although it seems your bird has lost his head or a leg, he's fine. Sleeping on one foot with his head tucked under his wing (actually with his head turned about 180 degrees, and his beak tucked into the feathers on the back of his neck) is a normal sleeping position for many parrots although it looks a bit unusual or uncomfortable to bird owners. Be aware, too, that your bird will occasionally perch on one leg while resting the other.

Conures also fall asleep in their food bowls, often on their backs with their feet in the air. You may fear your bird has died the first time you see him do this. But some conures routinely sleep on their backs. As long as he appears healthy, eats well, and acts normally, you have no cause for concern if your conure sleeps on his back. Some parent birds even feed their chicks when the babies are lying on their backs, so it's an entirely comfortable position for a conure to be in.

Bath Time

Conures are also great bathers. They'll try to bathe in their water bowls if nothing else is available, but they prefer to be dunked under the water faucet or to stand under a light shower in the kitchen sink. Be sure the water is lukewarm before letting your conure take a quick dip, and allow plenty of time for your bird's feathers to dry before he goes to bed (a blow dryer set on low can accelerate the drying process).

Escape Artists

Finally, conures can be excellent escape artists, so make sure the cage you select for your conure is completely secure and that the door and cage grill are not prone to popping open or falling out. Make sure the food and water bowl openings have covers that you can slide into place to help keep your pet in his cage while you're changing the bowls. Check to make sure all windows in your home have screens on them, and doors to the outside world are closed tightly before you let your conure out of his cage.

Chapter 2. Why keep a conure?

Below are reasons why individuals opt to keep conures:

Companionship

The global census tells us that more people than ever are living alone. A friendly whistle and a bit of a talk in the morning may be just what you need to shake off some loneliness. Sharing an ordinary breakfast with a conure offers you moments of genuine affection and reassurance.

Your bird may ask to have his beak stroked or to go to your finger so that you can provide him with bites of your own breakfast, which will be infinitely more interesting than whatever you planned to feed him.

Before heading out for a very busy day, having a few minutes just to talk things over as you change the paper and exchange yesterday's water for a fresh supply can be gratifying. This may be one of the high points of your day—just the morning routine.

Conures love their routines, and their needs help give our own lives stability and meaning. By providing for his needs in the way of food, toys, social interaction, and a clean, well-lit place to live, you enjoy the daily constancy of a relationship.

For people who have few demands in their lives, a companion bird provides a focus and a purposeful routine of care, feeding, and interaction. Sometimes, life with your conure will be an unbelievably rewarding experience.

Link to the Wild

For some of us, conures provide a link to the wild that is otherwise missing in life. While living and working in cities or suburbs, we long to be elsewhere, living in a remote place filled with trees and the calls of monkeys and birds. In other words, the fact that a conure is not a domestic animal, molded through thousands of generations of selective breeding to fit in with our lives, is exactly what we're looking for. Before we head out for work, we'd like to be reminded that there is something else in the world, something not quite so civilized as our version of life.

Lifetime Fascination

Some of us cannot stop admiring the beauty, the wonder, and the complexity of wild birds. We have to have birds in our lives. We cannot imagine life without birds as an integral part of every day. We realize that we not only need to have birds in our lives, but we work to preserve birds in their natural habitats so that their species can flourish.

These are the people who join various national and international associations to support research into understanding companion and wild birds, and who promote their health and welfare, associating with others who also cannot stay away from these sometimes raucous companions. Even when our conures are stubborn, we remember that they are doing what they've evolved to do (at least we remember that most of the time!). What makes them difficult is also what makes learning about them so satisfying.

Other Reasons

Conures have been companions of humans for thousands of years; for many Native People, these birds' feathers provide essential elements for religious ceremonies.

For many others, conures' ability to mimic speech or sounds is an attraction. Whatever the reason you fall in love with these birds, there is likely a species that will suit you and your living situation, if you are willing to provide what that bird needs.

Why Not Keep a conure?

There are many reasons not to keep a conure. The trick is to anticipate them and decide whether you are a conure person. If you love antiques and oriental carpets and covet the perfect looks from Architectural Digest, a conure is not for you. You will resent the mess, the non-designer cages, and the bird paraphernalia. If you love the obedience of dogs but want the colors of a conure, get a poodle and have your groomer sculpt and color his hair. Do not expect a conure to be obedient. If you want another pet but feel you don't have much time, a conure is a poor choice.

The Worst Possible Scenario

Whenever I try to explain why one might not want to have a conure, I suggest the following scenario: Imagine a two-year-old who will never grow up and out of the "No!" phase. Now, give the little tyke a small chainsaw (if you don't believe that is a fair comparison for a beak on a bored conure, you haven't spent enough time with parrots). Finally, imagine that the chainsaw-wielding two-year-old can fly.

Now, a budgerigar is a bird with a teeny-tiny chainsaw that is targeted toward paper and other easily chewed items like the pages of cookbooks or knitting patterns. A scarlet macaw, on the other hand, can crack a 1 × 1-inch piece of wood with a single closing of his beak. To be a successful conure companion, you have to be an anticipatory, a bad-behavior preventer, and a person who can swoop in and present the feathered two-year-old with something so interesting that he is no longer interested in cracking the leg on your antique chair or chasing after your sister's newly pedicured scarlet toes.

If Decor Is Important

Also, the larger parrots require large accommodations. If you are a person who values flawless carpets and Japanese wood-carved figures, think again before considering a conure as a pet. To the bird, everything in his environment is for chewing, tasting, pulling apart, and examining. Most conures are jungle natives.

Their ecological role is as a spreader of partially digested seeds and a provider of uneaten plant parts and nutrients that serve as fertilizer. This evolved behavior will not change because you have brought a conure into your home. Although there are cases of people potty training their birds, in general, this approach does not work well for a variety of reasons. Inevitably, your most valuable and rare figurines will be the ones that attract your conure's attention, and you'll need to put them behind glass or in an enclosed display area out of your conure's way.

Do You Value Obedience?

Unlike domestic animals, birds have no interest in pleasing you. Training a conure is a bit like training a cat. You have to find a way to appeal to the conure's higher want. The trouble is that, without quite a bit of experience, this is much more difficult than training a dog. If you do want to train your conure, there are simple approaches that work. The issue is that you must follow the experts' directions because nothing about training your bird is intuitive. This is all practice, repetition, and patience in rewarding minimal improvements.

To enjoy having a conure as a companion, you have to be able to put aside your ideas about what is acceptable behavior and find a way to coexist with an animal who evolved in the treetops, to live in flocks, and to spend a majority of the day foraging for food. If you cannot provide either these conditions or conditions that mimic the parrots' natural environment in these critical ways, your life together will not be as happy as you both would wish life to be.

Family Cooperation
One of the most practical bird behaviorists in recent years is Liz Wilson. Her advice about the difficulties of having a conure as a companion is that not all household members are enthusiastic about living with a bird. Because conures can be so difficult, for the relationship to be successful, it is essential for everyone in the home to be enthusiastic about the prospect.

Everyone in the family will need to handle the bird, keep the same rules, and cooperate with one another in conure related responsibilities. This cooperation begins before acquiring a bird. If everyone is not enthusiastic, then acquiring a bird is a mistake. The placement will not be a success.

Why Conures Lose Their Homes
Concerned about the number of birds losing their homes, avian veterinarians studied the reasons that conures are given up for adoption. Among the unanticipated reasons that conures are relinquished to adoption agencies or abandoned include "changes in the family structure such as deaths, divorces, financial difficulties and moving into places that do not accommodate pets, etc." However, in addition to those problems that cannot be foreseen, many parrots are given up because their owners' expectations have not been met by the bird or because new conure owners become either bored with their new pet or upset because the conure has not behaved well.

They found that although "not enough time" was reported most frequently as the reason for relinquishing birds, further questioning revealed that "dissatisfaction with the relationship," "unfulfilled expectations," or "inability of the owner to communicate to the conure their wants and needs" played a significant role. They believe that although the incompatibility issues that lead to negative behaviors such as aggression, noisiness, and feather destruction could be resolved through training and enrichment, in many cases the relationship between bird and owner had already deteriorated past repair.

To Make Good Matches, Education is Key
These researchers concluded that the most important way to keep conures in their original homes is to educate the prospective parrot owner about "appropriate bird choice and reasonable expectations." Surprisingly, they found that "many [conure] purchases are impulse buys." Your reading of this book is an excellent first step in learning about what type of conure might work as a member of your family and what you should expect to do to keep your bird happy and healthy.

Among many other educational opportunities, you can explore local bird club meetings, online communities, and visit specialty veterinarians or rescue organizations.

For every family that has a negative experience with conures, you can find families who treasure their avian companions and who go to great lengths to ensure they are well cared for and have everything a companion bird could want. These conure lovers gather at local and national meetings, through online communities, and at their local bird specialty stores and behavioral seminars. If you've never visited an avian veterinarian's office, you'd be surprised at the number of people who create friendships there in the lobby waiting for their bird check-ups or talking about the concerns they have for a bird who needs treatment.

As with any other special interest, people who love birds have an instant affinity for one another. We understand their worries, their difficulties in getting the best veterinarian for their bird, their need for that expensive puzzle toy that will keep their bird busy while they are on the telephone, the concern they have in the spring when some birds become more difficult because of their reproductive hormones, their worry when a bird begins to barber or pluck his feathers. These are concerns that those who do not have conures find difficult to understand.

If you decide that a parrot is right for you, I will urge you to join with some more informed conure owners who will be glad to share their knowledge and help you begin your long and fascinating journey into the world of the conure.

With so many species to choose from, each with slightly different anatomies, different dietary needs, behavioral quirks, and challenges, as well as their own endearing qualities, you may be able to find a conure who fits your lifestyle, your home style, and your personal style. If you cannot, many opportunities exist for you to volunteer to spend your time with birds while not taking full responsibility for an individual conure for his lifetime.

These opportunities include local rescue groups and humane societies, bird clubs, and events that support behaviorists and researchers as well as companion parrot owners. There may even be opportunities for you to work regularly with a parrot person who lives near you.

Costs of parrot ownership

Conures aren't cheap. After the cost of the bird itself, housing is the next most expensive proposition on the list and can be more costly than the bird. Here are some basic costs:

Conure: $15 to $30,000 / £12 to £23,000
Housing: $150 to $3,000 / £120 to £,2300 to sky's the limit
Accessories: Toys, perches, and so on can run $30 to $250 / £24 to £195 or more
Food: $25 to $75 / £20 to £60 monthly — more if you buy organic
Supplements: $50 to $150 / £40 to £120 monthly
Veterinary care: $200 to $1,000 / £155 to £776 or more per year
Time off work to spend with your bird: Priceless
Note: currency conversions can vary.

Responsibilities of conure guardianship

There's no such thing as a low-maintenance conure. That's what a lot of people ask for when they walk into a pet shop: "Which one is easy to take care of?" Well, I will admit that it's easier to take care of a pair of birds who love each other — for example, male and female parakeets, lovebirds, parrotlets, cockatiels, and others (the small and small/medium birds). If these birds have the proper spacious housing and care, they don't need any human interaction other than feeding, cleaning, and veterinary care. As for a "family conure," the low maintenance idea is out.

The sad fact is that many birds get shuffled to another home about every two to five years. It's not so much that conure parents are lazy about proper care; it's more that information about proper avian nutrition and medicine is just not getting to the general public. Birdkeepers have known for many years that you can't just feed conures seeds and water and expect them to thrive.

Even so, the majority of food seen in pet shops is still seeded or seed based, but that's changing. As an alternative, manufacturers began to make pellets, claiming that they're a whole diet for birds, the way kibble is a whole diet for dogs. Neither all-seed nor all-pellet diets are truly whole. Fortunately, people who have had birds a long time have come up with pretty good dietary regimens for birds, though nothing's perfect. The "right" diet for a conure takes a lot of effort — buying a multitude of the correct kinds of items, chopping, cooking, peeling, and so on.

Chapter 3: All types of Conures

There are twenty-five conures you might encounter in pet stores, at bird shows, or during your visits to bird breeders. Hopefully, one of them will prove to be the perfect pet for you!

In the descriptions that follow, the scientific names are provided to help you distinguish between the species. Some books classify conures by their common North American names, while others call them by their common British names.

But the scientific names are the same no matter where in the world you go, so they will assist you in determining which conure is which.

1. *Austral Conure (Enicognathus ferrugineus)*
In her native habitat of southern Chile, the austral conure has the distinction of being the southernmost parrot in the wild. He measures fourteen and a half inches long and weighs about five ounces. Australs were exported to Europe and the United States for more than 100 years, but they failed to catch on with breeders because of their dull coloration, so they might be difficult to find.

In captivity, these olive drab birds with black beaks, gray feet, and blackish-gray eye rings make quite good pets. They are less noisy than most conures, but they tend to vocalize in the evening.

Australs like to forage on the floor of their cage or aviary, looking for tubers, nuts, seeds, berries, and leaf buds. Although in general, bird owners should be concerned if they see their bird on the bottom of her cage all the time, this is perfectly normal behavior for an Austral conure and no cause for alarm. Austral owners do need to pay extra attention to the cleanliness of their pet's cage floor, however, because their bird will be spending more time down there than other species might.

2. *Aztec Conure* (Aratinga nana astec)
This conure, which many consider being a subspecies of the olive-throated conure, has green head feathers and olive-colored body feathers. Her beak is horn-colored and her feet are grey. Aztecs measure about ten inches long and weigh about three ounces. Their native range is from central Mexico to western Panama.

As pets, Aztecs are known for their talking ability, which is considered quite good for a conure. They are feisty little birds who charm everyone they meet. Somewhat rare as pets, they are worth the wait if you are looking for a small bird with a big personality.

3. Black-Capped Conure (Pyrrhura rupicola)
This uncommon conure has a black forehead, dark brown chest feathers that are scalloped in off-white, green belly feathers, and red feathers on the leading edge of her wings. The beak is gray, and the legs are dark gray. The black-cap measures about ten inches long and weighs about three ounces.

Black-caps were imported into the United States from southeastern Peru, northern Bolivia, and northwestern Brazil in extremely small numbers in the early 1980s. However, that small number of birds bred prolifically, so this little conure is now available as a pet.

4. Blue-Crown Conure (Aratinga acuticaudata)
As her name suggests, the blue-crown has a blue head and blue facial feathers. The coloring becomes more intense as the bird matures. Her body feathers are primarily green, the undersides of her wings are yellowish-green, and her tail feathers have reddish undersides. This bird has a horn-colored beak, white eye rings that are featherless, and pinkish feet.

Blue-crowns measure about fourteen and a half inches long and weigh about seven ounces. They were first bred in captivity in Great Britain in the early 1970s. In the wild, they are found in South America, from Venezuela to Argentina.

Blue-crowns, which are sometimes called sharp-tailed conures, can be noisy (especially if they are surprised or excited), but they are reasonably peaceful birds. They are popular as pets. They have the ability to talk and have friendly personalities.

5. Brown-Throated Conure (Aratinga pertinax)
This wonderful little conure has an orangish face, green wing and body feathers, buff-colored eye rings, a black beak, and gray legs. He measures about nine and a half inches long and weighs about four ounces. He was imported into St. Thomas in the Virgin Islands about 125 years ago and is sometimes called the St. Thomas conure. He is also found in Central and South America, from Panama to Brazil.

Some conure fanciers believe brown-throats make great pets, while others are quick to point out that these birds can be aggressive, destructive, and noisy. As with all creatures, each brown-throat has her personality. To determine whether he's the right bird for you, spend some time with a brown-throated conure before deciding to own one.

6. Cactus Conure (*Aratinga cactorum*) These conures from northeastern Brazil have a gray forehead and throat feathers, a yellowish belly, and green wings. Their beaks are horn colored, their eye rings are white, and their feet are black. Cactus conures measure about ten inches long and weigh about three ounces. The bird's common name comes from the fact that cactus fruit comprises a large part of her diet.

Cactus conures can become affectionate pets. They are easily tamed, are not destructive, and tend to be quieter than some other conures. Unfortunately, Brazil did not export many of these birds, so these little charmers are not common as pets. Some breeders are starting to raise them in captivity.

7. Cherry-Headed Conure (*Aratinga erythrogenys*)
Sometimes called the red-headed or red-masked conure, mature cherry-heads have red facial feathers; green body feathers with a sprinkling of red on the throat, shoulders, and thighs; bare white eye rings; horn-colored beaks; and dark gray legs. Mature cherry-heads are about thirteen inches long and weigh between five and seven ounces.

Young cherry-heads are predominantly green until their first molts, and older birds can take up to ten years to fully develop their red plumage. In the wild, cherry heads are found in a narrow range in western Ecuador and Peru.

Cherry-heads can learn to talk, and if they do, they often opt to speak their owners' language instead of vocalizing in conure speech. Cherry-heads are popular as pets.

8. Dusky Conure (*Aratinga weddelli*)
Sweetness seems to be a hallmark of this commonly kept small conure, which is sometimes called Weddell's conure. Other adjectives used to describe her include calm, gentle, and mellow. He is not an eye-catching bird, being mostly green with a gray-blue head, white eye rings, and a black beak and feet, but her affectionate personality soon wins hearts.

Conure fanciers routinely describe her as quiet, which is not an adjective often used to describe a conure. A dusky conure can also learn to talk, which may win her even more fans. Duskies measure about eleven inches long and weigh about four ounces. In the wild, they are found from southeastern Colombia to western Brazil.

9. Finsch's Conure (Aratinga finschi)
These popular pet birds bear a striking resemblance to the red-fronted, or Wagler's conure, but Finsch's conures have red feathers on the front edges of their wings.
Their body feathers are mostly green, their beaks are horn colored, their eye rings are creamy white, and they have gray-brown legs and feet. Mature Finsch's conures measure about eleven inches long and weigh about six ounces.

As with the cherry-heads, young Finsch's conures are completely green. As they mature, they develop their characteristic red foreheads. The native range for the Finsch's conure is southern Nicaragua to western Panama.

10. Gold-Capped Conure (Aratinga auricapilla)
This commonly kept conure has a golden-orange forehead, a green chest, and a reddish belly. Her eye rings are white, her beak is grey-black, and her legs are grey.

The gold-cap measures about twelve inches long and weighs about five ounces. He is a common pet bird in the United States. Gold-caps, sometimes called golden-headed conures, are prone to lying on their backs in their food bowls or their owners' hands—it's simply a comfortable position for them.

They are active, energetic little birds and have been captive bred in the United States since the early 1980s. Although they are not as flashy as the yellow-orange jenday or sun conures, some conure experts believe the gold-cap makes the least amount of noise and has the best pet potential of this golden trio.

11. Green-Cheeked Conure (Pyrrhura molinae)
Sometimes the Green-cheeked and the maroon-bellied conures are confused with each other. Although recent DNA analysis suggests they may, in fact, be the same species, I will nonetheless treat them separately. The green-cheeked conure and the maroon-bellied are both popular pets, and they do resemble each other quite closely.

Both birds have brown heads, green cheek feathers, brown chest feathers scalloped with buff or yellow, maroon belly and tail feathers, white eye rings, gray beaks, and dark gray legs. But the Green-cheeked has a darker brown head, less maroon on her belly, greener on her cheeks, and a lighter background on the barred area on the chest feathers. The green-cheeked also has an entirely maroon tail.

In the wild, the green-cheeked is found in west central Brazil, northern Bolivia, and northwestern Argentina. He measures about ten inches long and weighs about four ounces. Green-cheeks make engaging, bold, and inquisitive pets. They lack the loud voice of an Aratinga, so their vocalizations should be tolerable for most owners.

12. Half-Moon Conure (Aratinga canicularis)
The half-moon, or Petz's conure, is often confused with the peach-fronted conure. Half-moon conures have orange foreheads, olive chest feathers, green wing and belly feathers, horn-colored beaks (as opposed to the peach fronts black beak), orange-yellow eye rings (the peach fronts eye ring has small orange feathers on it), and dark gray feet. Half-moons measure nine and a half inches long and weigh about two and a half ounces.

The half-moon conure may be the best known of the Aratinga species because he was widely imported from western Central America for some years.

Since the 1970s, half-moons have been bred in captivity in the United States. Young half-moons are as bold as brass. These fearless birds can learn to talk, and they make tame, affectionate pets.

13. Jenday Conure (Aratingajandaya)
Almost as colorful as the sun conure, the jenday is an eye-catching bird. He has predominantly orange-red body feathers, green wings with blue accent feathers, white eye rings, a black beak, and blackish feet. Jendays measure about twelve inches long and weigh about five ounces.

Since the early 1980s; breeders have been able to meet the needs of pet owners with domestically bred birds. Although they can be somewhat noisy, jendays make inquisitive, acrobatic pets.

14. Maroon-Bellied Conure (Pyrrhura frontalis)
Like her green-cheeked relative, the maroon-bellied conure has a brown head, green cheek feathers, brown chest feathers scalloped with buff or yellow, a maroon belly and tail feathers, white eye rings, a grey beak, and dark grey legs.

In contrast to the Green-cheeked, the Maroon-bellied, as her name suggests, has a larger patch of maroon belly feathers, more yellow on her chest, and green head feathers. Maroon-bellied measure about ten inches long and weigh about three ounces.

Maroon-bellied, which may also be called scaly-breasted conures, were imported into the United States and Europe from their native ranges in southeastern Brazil, Uruguay, Paraguay, and northern Argentina starting in the 1920s. The species has since been set up in captive breeding programs, and pairs have done quite well in producing chicks.

Maroon-bellied have large personalities in their small bodies, and they make lively, playful pets.

15. Maroon-Tailed Conure (Pyrrhura melanura)
This bird also goes by the name black-tailed conure. He measures about nine and a half inches long and weighs about three ounces. The maroon-tailed has a brown forehead; green cheeks, wing and belly feathers; and brown-green chest feathers that are scalloped with white.

The maroon-tailed also has red feathers on the leading edges of her wings. Her eye rings are white, and her beak and feet are gray. As you might expect, her tail feathers are black on top and maroon on the underside, which gives rise to both of her common names.

In the wild, maroon-tailed conures are found from southern Venezuela to northeastern Peru. Maroon-tailed make entertaining pets, and they are not hard to find.

They enjoy being around people and talk to strangers rather quickly, winning new friends with their charming personalities.

16. Mitred Conure (Aratinga mitrata)
Mitred conures are primarily green with rings, horn-colored beaks, and brown legs. As with other green and red conures discussed here, young mitreds are completely green until their first molt, when the red forehead starts to become evident. Mitreds are fifteen inches long and weigh about eight and a half ounces.

Mitred conures can be very affectionate, but they're also loud.

Mitreds became well known to pet owners when importing birds was at its height; thousands of these parrots were brought into the United States from the mitred's native habitat, which stretches from central Peru to northwestern Argentina. Their popularity is even greater with the introduction of domestically bred birds.

Although mitreds can be quite vocal, they are also very affectionate pets. This loyal affection for their owners has won the species many fans over the years. They also like to chew, so be sure your mitred has lots of toys he can destroy.

17. Nanday Conure (Nandayus nenday)
One of the more colorful conure species, the nanday, has a black forehead and cheeks, bluish throat, green belly and wing feathers, orange leg feathers, white eye rings, black beak, and pink feet. Nandays, which are also known as black-headed or black-masked conures, are twelve inches long and weigh about five ounces.

Nandays were exported from their native habitat, which ranges from southeastern Bolivia to northern Argentina, for more than a hundred years. As is the case with many wild-caught parrots, wild nandays developed a reputation as poor pets.

Today's hand-fed, domestically bred nandays, however, are difficult to top. They are naturally social birds who thrive on attention from their owners, and they get along well with other parrots. The nanday's main drawback as a pet is that some of them can be quite loud, so they may not be well-suited for life in an apartment or a town house.

It's difficult to be indifferent about a nanday because these acrobatic little extroverts quickly charm their way into your heart. Many nanday owners are extremely loyal to their colorful little friends. First-time owners need to remember that nandays tend to fall asleep on their backs with their feet in the air—a behavior that can be alarming the first time you see it.

18. Patagonian Conure (*Cyanoliseus patagonus*)

This is the largest conure, measuring about seventeen and a half inches long and weighing a little more than half a pound. Although some might describe their plumage as dull, Patis are quite colorful with their olive heads, orange and yellow bellies, blue flight feathers, pink feet, black beaks, and white eye rings. The natural range for this conure is central Chile, northern and central Argentina, and southern Uruguay.

In the wild, Patagonians are known to be ground feeders, so don't be alarmed if your Pati spends a lot of time on the bottom of her cage. As long as the bird appears otherwise healthy, this is a natural behavior. Patis are quite cuddly pets, and some can become good talkers. They have bred readily in captivity and are not hard to find. Among the drawbacks to keeping these conures is the fact that they can be quite loud, they require large cages to be comfortable, and they are voracious chewers.

19. Peach-Fronted Conure (*Aratinga aurea*)

Sometimes called the Golden-crowned conure, the peach-fronted conure can be easily confused with the half-moon. Peach-fronts have deep orange foreheads, olive throats, yellow belly feathers, and green wing feathers. Their beaks and feet are black, and their eye rings are covered with small orange feathers.

The Peach-fronted occupies a wide range—southern Brazil to northern Argentina—in her native habitat. He measures about ten inches long and weighs about four ounces.

Bird owners and breeders have kept Peach-fronted Conures for more than a hundred years. As pets, these conures have relatively good talking abilities and sweet dispositions. However, they can be destructive, noisy, and aggressive toward other parrots during the breeding season.

20. Queen of Bavaria Conure (*Aratinga guarouba*)

The Queen of Bavaria is a large, visually striking bird. Her primary feather color is a brilliant yellow with olive green flight feathers, and he has a horn-colored beak, white eye rings, and pinkish feet. Queens measure about fourteen inches long and weigh about half a pound. Because they are so eye-catching, they have been featured in advertisements for premium bird foods.

The San Diego Zoo has a pair of Queens on display that I make a point of visiting each time I'm there. These large conures cause more than a few visitors to stop and take a second look. Queens, which are sometimes called golden conures, are native to a small area in northeastern Brazil.

They are endangered in the wild because of deforestation, nest site destruction, and human encroachment. They have a long history of captive breeding that dates from 1939 in Sri Lanka. This species has been bred in the United States for more than fifty years. Despite this long history in captivity, Queens are uncommon pets, and they command top dollar.

Queens are prone to a few behavioral problems, including loud vocalization, feather picking, and aggression toward other parrots, particularly during breeding season. However, they are generally tame and affectionate toward their owners.

This species is not recommended for first-time conure owners because they require a great deal of attention and because they are still not common in aviculture. Queen of Bavaria conures are big, affectionate birds. However, they are also prone to behavior problems and are not a good choice for the first-time bird owner.

21. (Aratinga wagleri) Red-Fronted Conure
Also known as Wagler's conure, the red-fronted is a green bird with a red forehead, white eye rings, a horn-colored beak, and brownish feet. Young birds start out life completely green and develop their red foreheads as they mature. The red-fronted is about fourteen and a half inches long and weighs about six and a half ounces.

In the wild, the red-fronted conure's native range stretches in a narrow band from northern Venezuela to southern Peru. These birds have been bred in captivity in the United States since 1957. They make entertaining pets and are capable of learning a variety of tricks.

22. Red-Throated Conure (Aratinga holochlora rubritorquis)
This subspecies of the green conure makes a comical pet who has a good chance of becoming a talking bird. Red-throated conures measure about twelve inches long and weigh about four ounces.

In the wild, red-throated are found from eastern Guatemala to northern Nicaragua. Across their range, these birds are highly prized as pets. They were not imported to the United States in large numbers, but the birds who are here have bred well in captivity.

Red-throated conures don't develop their red feathers until after their first molt.

Like some other types of conures, young red-throated conures start out life all green (well, once they have their feathers, anyway). They develop their red throats after their first molt. Red-throats also have beige eye rings, horn-colored beaks, and brownish legs.

23. Slender-Billed Conure (Enicognathus leptorhynchus)
Like the austral, this olive drab conure with gray eye rings, a reddish stripe of feathers around her eyes, a black beak, and grayish feet has been largely overlooked in the pet trade because he simply doesn't have eye-catching plumage. This uncommon bird does, however, have an eye-catching beak that may cause some first-time bird owners to think something is wrong with her.

Her upper mandible is considerably longer than that of other parrots, but it's simply an adaptation that enables the slender-billed conure to dig for tubers and roots in her native habitat of central Chile.

The elongated bill also helps the bird retrieve one of her favorite foods— the seeds of the Araucaria araucana tree. Slender-billed conures kept in captivity might appreciate pine nuts, which are similar to their favorite wild seeds.

Slender-billed conures, which are sometimes called long-billed conures, are one of the larger conures, measuring about sixteen inches long and weighing about six ounces. They are peaceful birds who do well in captivity. They can be quite noisy when they want to be, but they can also learn to talk rather well.

Slender-billed tend to spend long periods of time on the cage floor, foraging for food, so don't be alarmed if your slender-billed seems to be down in her cage bottom all the time. You can make the hunt for food more interesting for this bird by scattering a few seeds in the bottom of her cage. Be alert to the condition of the cage bottom and keep it scrupulously clean to help ensure the health of your conure.

24. Sun Conure (Aratinga solstitialis)
These flashy little birds have been described as the Cadillacs of the conure group. A mature sun conure is a brilliant blaze of orange, yellow, red, and green feathers, and younger sun conures have mottled green plumage until their first molt. Mature suns have black beaks, white eye rings, and grayish feet. They measure about twelve inches long and weigh about four and a half ounces.

Suns are found in the wild from Guyana to northeastern Brazil, but they have been captive bred in the United States for many years. As pets, they are known for being content to be with their owners for hours at a time, sitting on a shoulder or the back of a chair. They can be noisy if ignored but otherwise make fine pets.

25. White-Eyed Conure (Aratinga leucophthalmus)
White-eyed conures are affectionate birds and may learn to talk when they are still quite young.

White-eyed conures take their name from the bare ring of white skin around their eyes. They are predominantly green birds with a sprinkling of red on their bodies, horn-colored beaks, and gray-brown legs. White-eyed conures measure about thirteen inches long and weigh about four and a half ounces.

In the wild, white-eyed conures can be found from Guyana to Uruguay. They have bred well in captivity and are commonly available as pets. They can be quite affectionate, engaging birds and may learn to talk at a quite early age.

Chapter 4. Choosing the Right Conure for You

Before I decided to bring a conure into my life, I considered a few questions.

Do I like animals?

Do I have the time to care for one properly?

Can I have pets where I live?

Can I live with a little mess (seed hulls, feathers, and discarded food) in my home?

Can I tolerate, and appreciate, a little noise (the kind made by an excited conure) as part of my daily routine?

After answering yes to all these questions, I considered myself a good candidate for bird ownership. And my next question was, "Why do I want a bird?" Here are some of the answers.

Why Choose a Bird?

Birds' small size makes them good pets for today's smaller living spaces. More individuals are living in apartments, mobile or manufactured homes, or condominiums, which makes it awkward and inconvenient to keep a large pet who needs a yard and lots of regular exercise. Birds just seem to fit better in apartments, condos, mobile homes, and other smaller living spaces.

For instance, I am a bird owner who rents an apartment, but my current landlord has written a letter of reference for my future landlord, for my birds that I can use to show how responsible I am as a bird owner and how well behaved my bird has been. In many rental leases, birds may not even be considered pets because they are kept in a cage much of the time. This means you may be able to keep them without having to surrender a sizable security deposit to a landlord.

Birds interact well with their owners. Although a bird isn't as blindly loyal as the average dog, he is far more interactive than a fish, a hamster, or even a guinea pig. As a bonus, many birds can learn to whistle or talk, which is unique among pets and which many bird owners find amusing and entertaining.

Birds require consistent, but not constant, attention. This can be a plus for today's busy single people and families. Although birds can't be ignored all day, they are content to entertain themselves for part of the day while their owners are busy elsewhere.

The needs and companionship of a bird provide a reason to get up in the morning. The value of this cannot be overestimated for older bird owners and single people who are on their own. Birds provide all the benefits of the human animal bond, including lower blood pressure and reduced levels of stress.

Finally, birds are intelligent pets. Whoever coined the phrase "bird brain" didn't appreciate how smart some birds are. On intelligence tests, some larger parrots have scored at levels comparable to chimpanzees, dolphins, and preschool-age children.

Where Will You Get Your Conure?
I got my conure from a bird breeder, who advertised the bird in a bird specialty magazine, You can also get them from the pet section of your newspaper's classified ads, at bird shows, or from bird specialty stores. Let's look at each in a bit more detail.

Classified Ads
Private parties usually place classified ads. If the advertiser offers young birds, you've found a private breeder who wants to place a few birds in good homes. Most pet conures can leave the breeder's home at around three months of age.

Some breeders may also offer older birds for sale from time to time. These are most likely breeder birds who are too old to produce chicks but who would still make good pets.

Bird Shows
Shows offer bird breeders and bird buyers an opportunity to get together to share a love of birds. Bird shows can give you the chance to see many different types of birds all in one place, which can help you narrow your choices if you're undecided about which species to keep. At a bird show, you can watch to see which birds win consistently and then talk to the breeder of these birds after the show to see if they expect any chicks.

Bird Specialty Stores
Specialty stores might be the ideal place to purchase a conure. If a store in your area sells conures, you'll need to visit and make sure it's clean and well kept. Walk around the store a bit. Do the cages look and smell like they're cleaned regularly?

Do the birds in the cages appear to be alert, well fed, and healthy? Do the cages appear crowded or do the animals inside have some room to move around?

Look at the birds available for sale. If possible, sit down and watch them for a while. Don't rush this important step. Do some of them seem bolder than the others? Consider those first, because you want a curious, active, robust pet, rather than a shy animal who hides in a corner.

If possible, let your conure choose you. Many bird stores display their animals on T-stands or play gyms, or a breeder may bring out a clutch of babies for you to look at. If one bird waddles right up to you and wants to play, or if one comes over to check you out and just seems to want to come home with you, that's the bird for you!

The Preowned Parrot

You may see adult birds advertised for sale at a bird store or in the newspaper. Adopting an adult conure could be a great mistake if the bird has behavioral problems, or it could be the best investment you'll ever make.

People put adult conures up for sale for many reasons. Perhaps the bird detects stress in the home and begins to pull his feathers, and the owners have neither the time nor the patience to solve the problem. The owners may have a child and suddenly no longer have time for the parrot, or they may be moving and cannot take their pet with them. Some people simply lose interest in their birds and sell them after a few years.

If you want to consider a preowned parrot, make an appointment to see the bird in his current home. Ask why the owners are selling the bird and see whether you and the bird "click" on a personal level.

Ownership Challenges

An awareness of the behavioral quirks of conures will help you better prepare for them, and may help you decide whether a conure is really the right bird for you.

First, conures are noted chewers, which means they will need an abundant supply of sturdy toys that can be destroyed. If you don't provide them with proper chewing stimulation, they will find it in other places in your home, such as your entryway banister and the houseplants. Be sure to supervise your conure when he is out of his cage to prevent him from chewing on inappropriate and potentially harmful things.

Next, conures can and will vocalize, and many of them can be quite loud. Members of the Aratinga genus of conures are louder than those of the Pyrrhura genus, but that's only a general rule and exceptions abound. (The first part of the scientific name of the conures described in chapter 2, "All Types of Conures" tells you which genus they belong to.) To help make sure you get a relatively quiet conure, buy a hand-fed bird who has been properly socialized by the breeder. This means the breeder paid individual attention to every chick and took the time to handle and play with them.

Is This Conure Healthy?

Here are some of the signs that a conure is healthy. I always keep them in mind when am selecting my pet, and reject any birds who do not meet these criteria.

• Bright eyes
• Clean cere (the area above the bird's beak that covers his nares, or nostrils)
• Clean legs and vent
• Smooth feathers
• Upright posture
• Quiet breathing
• Full-chested appearance
• Bird is actively moving around the cage
• Good appetite

Remember that healthy birds spend their time doing three main activities—eating, playing, and sleeping—in about equal amounts of time. If you notice a bird who seems only to want to sleep, for instance, reject that bird in favor of another whose routine seems more balanced.

If your conure seems curious about the world around him and trusting of new people, chances are excellent that he was well-socialized by his breeder. You will need to continue this process by playing with your parrot and helping him explore his new environment (your home) in a safe, secure way.

Once your conure comes home with you, you should give him regular periods of attention and lots of toys to play with when you aren't around. By doing this, you should be able to minimize any loud vocal outbursts.

Bringing Your Conure Home

Your new pet will need some time to adjust to his new environment, so be patient. Give your conure a chance to adjust to your family's routine gradually after you bring him home. After you set your conure up in his cage for the first time, spend a few minutes talking quietly to him, and use his name frequently while you're talking.

After a couple of days of adjustment, your conure should start to settle into his routine. You will be able to tell when your new pet has adjusted to your home because healthy and relaxed conures will spend about equal amounts of time during the day eating, playing and sleeping. By observation, you will soon recognize your pet's normal routine. You may also notice that your bird fluffs or shakes his feathers to greet you, or that he chirps a greeting when you uncover his cage in the morning.

Chapter 5. Home Sweet Home

Before you bring your feathered friend home, you have a lot of shopping to do. Selecting your conure's cage will be one of the most important decisions you make for him. You must also decide where he will live in your house or apartment. Don't wait until you bring your bird home to think this through. You'll want your new pet to settle in comfortably right away, rather than adding to his stress by relocating him several times before you decide on the right spot for the cage. That was my first step to owning a bird.

Here's what you'll need to look for to set your conure up right.

Choosing a Cage

When selecting a cage for your conure, make sure the bird has room to spread his wings without touching the cage sides. His tail should not touch the cage bottom, nor should his head brush the top. A cage that measures two feet by two feet by three feet is the minimum size for a single conure, and bigger is always better.

Check the Bars

Examine any cage you choose carefully before making your final selection. If you are choosing a cage with coated bars, make sure that the finish is not chipped, bubbled, or peeling, because your pet may find the defective spot and continue removing the finish, which can cause a cage to look old and worn before its time. Also, your pet could become ill if he ingests any of the finish.

If you are considering a galvanized wire cage, be aware that some birds can become ill from ingesting pieces of the galvanized wire. You can prevent this "new cage syndrome" by washing down the cage wires thoroughly with a solution of vinegar and water and then scrubbing the cage with a wire brush to loosen any stray bits of galvanized wire. Rinse the cage thoroughly with water and let it dry before putting your bird into his new home.

Reject any cages that have sharp interior wires or wide spaces between the bars. (Recommended bar spacing for conures is about half an inch.) Sharp wires could poke your bird, he could become caught between bars that are slightly wider than recommended, or he could escape through widely spaced bars. Also be aware that birds can injure themselves on ornate scrollwork that decorates some cages.

Finally, make sure the cage you choose has some horizontal bars in it so your conure can climb the cage walls easily for exercise.

Cage Door Options

After you've checked the overall cage quality and the bar spacing, look at the cage door. Does it open easily for you, yet remain secure enough to keep your bird in his cage when you close the door? Some conures become quite good at letting themselves out of their cage if the door does not close securely. If you discover you have a feathered Houdini on your hands, a small padlock may help keep your escape artist in his place.

Will your bird's food bowl or a bowl of bath water fit through the door easily? Is it long and wide enough for you to get your hand in and out of the cage comfortably—with the bird perched on your hand? Does the door open up, down, or to the side? Some bird owners like their pets to have a play porch on a door that opens out and down, drawbridge style, while others are happy with doors that open to the side. Watch out for guillotine-style doors that slide up and over the cage entrance, because some conures had suffered a broken leg when the door dropped on them unexpectedly.

Cage Tray Considerations

Next, look at the tray in the bottom of the cage. Does it slide in and out of the cage easily? Remember that you will be changing the paper in this tray at least once a day for the rest of your bird's life (which could be forty years, with good care). Is the tray an odd shape or size? Will paper need to be cut into unusual shapes to fit in it, or will paper towels, newspapers or clean sheets of used computer paper fit easily? The easier the tray is to remove and reline, the more likely you will be to change the lining of the tray daily. Can the cage tray be replaced if it becomes damaged and unusable?

You may notice that some of the cages for conures feature cage aprons, which help keep the debris your bird will create in a day off your floor and somewhat under control. Cage aprons make cleaning up after your bird quicker and easier, and they also protect your carpet or flooring from discarded food and bird droppings if your bird decides to perch on the edge of his cage.

Finally, check the floor of the cage you've chosen. Does it have a grill that will keep your bird out of the debris that falls to the bottom of the cage, such as feces, seed hulls, molted feathers, and discarded food? To ensure your pet's long-term good health and to protect your conure from his own curious nature, it's essential to have a grill between your pet and the debris

33

in the cage tray. Also, it's easier to keep your conure in his cage while you're cleaning the cage tray if there's a grill between the cage and the tray.

The Cage Cover

One important, but sometimes overlooked, accessory is the cage cover. Be sure you have something to cover your conure's cage with when it's time to put your bird to sleep each night. The act of covering the cage seems to calm many pet birds and convince them that it's time to go to bed, despite the sounds of an active family evening in the background.

Setting Up the Cage

Make sure you have the cage all set up and ready before you bring your bird home, to help ease the transition for your pet. Here's how to configure your conure's cage:

• Select the right location. Your conure will be more comfortable if his cage is set up in a part of the house that you and your family regularly use, such as a family room. Your conure's cage should be out of the main traffic flow of the room, but still be in the room so you can include your bird in normal activities, such as watching TV. (Don't put your bird's cage near the kitchen or the bathroom, because cooking and chemical fumes from these rooms can harm your conure.)

• Set the cage up with a solid wall behind it. Your conure will feel more secure if he has a solid wall behind his cage because nothing can sneak up on him from behind.

• Stagger the perches within the cage. Don't place the perches at all the same height in the cage because your conure will be happier if he can perch at different heights at different times of the day.

• Arrange the perches correctly. Don't place perches directly over food or water bowls because pet birds eliminate regularly during the day, and you don't want your pet's food or water contaminated by his droppings.

• Add some toys. Your conure will need toys in his cage to help entertain him during the day. You should rotate the toys regularly to ensure your bird doesn't become bored with the same toys. You'll also have to replace those that your pet destroys during playtime. Don't overfill the cage with toys because your bird still needs room to move around. He needs to climb around in the cage and maybe even take short flights from end to end for exercise. He also needs to be able to get to the food and water bowls without interference from his toys.

34

• Provide a cage cover. Your conure will benefit from having his cage covered when he goes to sleep at night. Covering the cage will help your bird settle down at bedtime, which helps him establish a good daily routine.

You can purchase a cage cover, or you can use an old sheet, blanket, or towel that is clean and free of holes. Be aware that some birds like to chew on their cage covers through the cage bars. If your bird does this, replace the cover when it becomes too tattered to do its job effectively. Replacing a well-chewed cover will also help keep your bird from becoming entangled in the cover or caught in a ragged clump of threads. Some birds have injured themselves quite severely by being caught in a chewed cage cover, so help keep your pet safe from this hazard.

What to Put in the Cage Tray

It is recommended that you use clean black-and-white newsprint, paper towels, or clean sheets of used computer printer paper. Sand, ground corncobs, or walnut shells may be sold by your pet supply store but are not recommended as cage flooring materials because they tend to hide feces and discarded food quite well.

This can cause a bird owner to forget to change the cage tray on the principle that if it doesn't look dirty, it must not be dirty. This line of thinking can set up a thriving, robust colony of bacteria in the bottom of your bird's cage, which can lead to a sick bird if you're not careful. Newsprint and other paper products don't hide the dirt; in fact, they seem to draw attention to it, which leads conscientious bird owners to keep their pets' homes scrupulously clean.

Place the cage where your conure will feel safe and comfortable but will still have plenty of interaction with your family.

You may see sandpaper or "gravel paper" sold in some pet stores as a cage tray liner. This product is supposed to provide a bird with an opportunity to ingest grit, which is reported to aid indigestion by providing coarse grinding material that helps break up food in the bird's gizzard. However, many avian experts do not believe that a pet bird needs grit, and if a bird stands on rough sandpaper, it could cause foot problems. For your pet's health, please don't use these gravel-coated papers.

Where to Put the Cage

Now that you've picked the perfect cage for your conure, where will you put it? Your conure will be happiest when he can feel like he's part of the family, so the living room, family room, or dining room may be among the best places for your bird.

Avoid keeping your bird in the bathroom or kitchen, because sudden temperature fluctuations or fumes from cleaning products used in those rooms could harm your pet. Another spot to avoid is a busy hall or entryway, because the activity level in these spots may be too much for your pet.

If possible, set up the cage so that it is at your eye level, because it will make servicing the cage and visiting your pet easier for you. It will also reduce the stress on your conure because birds like to be up high for security. Also, they do not like to have people or things looming over them, so consider items such as ceiling fans, chandeliers, or swag lamps. If members of your family are particularly tall, they may want to sit next to the cage or crouch down slightly to talk to the conure.

Whatever room you select for your conure's cage, be sure to put him in a secure corner (with one solid wall behind the cage to ensure his sense of security) and near a window. Please don't put the cage in direct sun, though, because conures can quickly overheat.

More to Buy
Along with the perfect size cage in the ideal location in your home, your conure will need a few cage accessories. These include food and water dishes, perches, and a play gym.

Dishes
Conures seem to enjoy food crocks, which are open ceramic bowls that allow them to hop up on the edge of the bowl and pick and choose what they will during the day. Crocks are also heavy enough to prevent mischievous birds from upending their food bowl, which can leave the bird hungry and you with quite a mess to clean up. You may also want to consider buying a cage with locking bowl holders because bowls that are locked in place (but are still easy to remove by you at mealtime) are less likely to be tipped over by your conure.

If your conure doesn't tip over his bowls, he may do well with a clean plastic tray from a frozen dinner or a metal pie plate. Be sure to buy dishes that are less than one inch deep to ensure that your bird has easy access to his food at all times. When buying dishes for your conure, be sure to pick up several sets so that mealtime cleanups are quick and easy.

36

Perches

When choosing perches for your pet's cage, try to buy two different diameters or materials so your bird's feet won't get tired of standing on the same-size perch of the same material day after day. Think of how tired your feet would feel if you stood on your bare feet on a piece of wood all day, then imagine how it would feel to stand on that piece of wood barefoot every day for years. Sounds pretty uncomfortable, doesn't it? That's basically what your bird has to look forward to if you don't vary his perching choices.

Birds spend all day on their feet and appreciate a variety of surfaces to stand and climb on.

The recommended diameter for conure perches is three-quarters of an inch, so try to buy one perch of that size and one that is slightly larger (one inch, for example) to give your pet a chance to stretch his foot muscles. Birds spend almost all of their lives standing, so keeping their feet healthy is important. Also, avian foot problems are much easier to prevent than they are to treat.

You'll probably notice a lot of different kinds of perches when you visit your pet supply store. Along with the traditional wooden dowels, bird owners can now buy perches made from manzanita branches, PVC tubes, rope perches, and terracotta or concrete grooming perches.

Manzanita offers birds varied diameters on the same perch, along with chewing possibilities, while PVC is almost indestructible. (Make sure any PVC perches you offer your bird have been scuffed slightly with sandpaper to improve traction).

Rope perches also offer varied diameters and a softer perching surface than wood or plastic, and terra cotta and concrete provide slightly abrasive surfaces that birds can use to groom their beaks without severely damaging the skin on their feet in the process.

However, some bird owners have reported that their pets have suffered foot abrasions with these perches. Watch your pet carefully for signs of sore feet (an inability to perch or climb, favoring a foot, or raw, sore skin on the feet) if you choose to use these perches in your pet's cage. If your bird shows signs of lameness, remove the abrasive perches immediately and arrange for your avian veterinarian to examine him.

When placing perches in your bird's cage, try to vary the heights slightly, so your bird has different levels in his cage. Don't place any perches over food or water dishes, because birds will contaminate food or water by eliminating in it. Finally, place one perch higher than the rest for a nighttime sleeping roost. Conures and other parrots like to sleep on the highest point they can find to perch, so please provide this security for your pet.

Choosing the Right Toys
Your new pet has an active, agile mind that needs regular stimulation and challenges. A bored bird is often a destructive, noisy bird—not an ideal pet. Toys for a conure can be as complex as you care to buy or as simple as an empty paper towel roll. When selecting toys for your bird, keep a few safety tips in mind.

Size
Is the toy the right size for your bird? Large toys can be intimidating to small birds, which makes the birds less likely to play with them. On the other end of the spectrum, larger birds can easily destroy toys designed for smaller birds, and they can sometimes injure themselves severely in the process. Select toys for your conure that are designed for small-to medium-size parrots to ensure they are the proper size for your conure.

Safety
Is the toy safe? Good choices include sturdy wooden toys (either undyed or painted with bird-safe vegetable dye or food coloring) strung on closed-link chains or vegetable-tanned leather thongs and rope toys. If you buy rope toys for your conure, make sure his nails are trimmed regularly to prevent them from snagging in the rope, and discard the toy when it becomes frayed to prevent accidents.

Unsafe items to watch out for are brittle plastic toys that can easily be shattered into fragments by a conure's busy beak, lead-weighted toys that can be cracked open to expose the dangerous lead to curious birds, loose link chains that can catch toenails or beaks, ring toys that are too small to climb through safely, and jingle-type bells that can trap toes, tongues, and beaks.

Don't assume every toy in the store is safe for your conure. Check for loose or brittle parts or toys that can catch a beak or a nail.

Conure Favorites
Conures kept as single pets sometimes enjoy mirrored toys. Make sure any mirrored toy you select is unbreakable because your conure's busy beak will give it quite a workout. If you notice that your conure is becoming

fixated on the pretty bird in the mirror, you should remove the mirrored toy and replace it with another safe, nonmirrored plaything.

Some entertaining toys can be made at home. Give your bird an empty paper towel roll or toilet paper tube (from unscented paper only, please), string some Cheerios on a piece of vegetable-tanned leather, or offer your bird a dish of raw pasta pieces to destroy.

Introducing New Toys

Conures are naturally curious, so introducing new toys to them should be a great adventure. You can set new toys next to your conure's cage to gauge his reaction. If he seems to want to know what the new item is, you can probably put it in the cage almost immediately. If your conure seems a bit apprehensive about the new toy, leave it by the cage for a few days to allow your pet to adjust to the presence of his new plaything.

Household Hazards

One of the reasons you chose a conure is because he's such a curious, active bird. These inquisitive little pets seem to be able to get into just about anything, which means they can get themselves into potentially dangerous situations rather quickly. Because of this natural curiosity, conure owners must be extremely vigilant when their birds are out of their cage.

Part of this vigilance should include bird-proofing your home. Parrot-proofing your home is akin to baby proofing it. Remember that some parrots are intellectually on a level similar to that of a toddler. You wouldn't let a toddler have free range of your house without taking precautions to safeguard the child from harm, and you should have the same concern for your conure.

Let's go room by room and look at some of the potentially dangerous situations you should be aware of.

Bathroom

This can be a conure paradise if the bird is allowed to spend time with you as you prepare for work or an evening out, but it can also be quite harmful to your bird's health. An open toilet could lead to drowning, the bird could hurt himself chewing on the electric cord of your blow-dryer, or he could be overcome by fumes from perfume, hairspray, or cleaning products, such as bleach, air freshener, and toilet bowl cleaner.

The bird could also become ill if he nibbles on prescription or nonprescription drugs in the medicine chest or he could injure himself by flying into a mirror. Use caution when taking your bird into the bathroom, and make sure his wings are clipped to avoid flying accidents.

Kitchen

This is another popular spot for birds and their owners to hang out, especially around mealtimes. Here again, dangers lurk for curious conures. An unsupervised bird could fly or fall into the trash can, or he could climb into the oven, dishwasher, freezer, or refrigerator and be forgotten. Your bird could land on a hot stove, or fall into an uncovered pot of boiling water or sizzling frying pan on the stove. The bird could also become poisoned by eating foods that are unsafe for him, such as chocolate, avocado, and rhubarb if they are left unattended on a countertop.

Living Room

Are you sitting on your couch or in a comfortable chair as you read this book? Although it probably seems safe enough to you, your pet could be injured or killed if he decides to play hide-and-seek under pillows or cushions and you accidentally sit on him. Your conure could become poisoned by nibbling on a leaded glass lampshade, or he could fly out an open window or patio door. He could also fly into a closed window or door and injure himself severely. He could become entangled in a drapery cord or a Venetian blind pull, he could fall into an uncovered fish tank and drown, or he could ingest poison by nibbling on ashes or cigarette butts in an ashtray.

Home Office

This can be another conure playground, but you'll have to be on your toes to keep your pet from harming himself by nibbling on potentially poisonous markers, glue sticks or crayons, and electrical cords, or impaling himself on push pins.

Other Areas of Concern

If you have a ceiling fan in your house, make sure it is turned off when your bird is out of his cage. Make sure you know where your bird is before turning on your washer or dryer and don't close your basement freezer without checking first to be sure your bird isn't in there. Lit candles, inlaid jewellery, sliding glass doors, and toxic houseplants also pose threats to your conure.

This doesn't mean you should keep your bird locked up in his cage all the time. On the contrary, all parrots need the time out of their cage to maintain physical and mental health. The key is to be aware of some of the dangers that may exist in your home and to pay attention to your bird's behavior, so you can intervene before the bird becomes ill or injured.

Nasty Fumes

Unfortunately, potential dangers to a pet bird don't stop with the furniture and accessories. A variety of fumes can overpower your conures, such as those from cigarettes, air fresheners, insecticides, bleach, shoe polish, oven cleaners, kerosene, lighter fluid, glues, active self-cleaning ovens, hairspray, overheated non-stick cookware, paint thinner, bathroom cleaners, and nail polish remover. Try to keep your pet away from anything that has a strong chemical odor, and be sure to apply makeup and hair care products far away from your conure.

To help protect your pet from harmful chemical fumes, consider using some "green" cleaning alternatives, such as baking soda and vinegar to clear clogged drains, baking soda instead of scouring powder to clean tubs and sinks, lemon juice and mineral oil to polish furniture, and white vinegar and water as a window cleaner. These products keep the environment a little friendlier for your bird, and these simple solutions to cleaning problems often work better than higher-priced, branded products.

Nonstick Cookware

Marathon cooking sessions may result in overheated cookware or stove top drip pans, which could kill your bird if the cookware or drip pans are coated with a non- stick finish. As it burns, toxic fumes are released that can kill a beloved pet bird.

You may want to consider replacing your nonstick cookware with stainless steel pots and pans, which you can treat with a nonstick cooking spray to make cleanups safe and easy. By the same token, the self-cleaning cycle on some ovens can create harmful fumes for pet birds. Use this cycle only if you have opened the windows around your bird's cage to let in fresh air. (Make sure your conure's cage is closed securely before opening a window).

Home Improvements

If you're considering a remodeling or home improvement project, think about your conure first. Fumes from paint or formaldehyde, which can be found in carpet backing, paneling, and particleboard, can cause pets and people to become ill. If you are having work done on your home, consider boarding your conure at your avian veterinarian's office or the home of a bird-loving friend or relative until the project is complete and the house is aired out. You can consider the house safe for your pet when you cannot smell any trace of any of the products used in the remodelling.

Pest Control

Having your home fumigated for termites poses another potentially hazardous situation for your pet conure. Ask your exterminator for information about the types of chemicals that will be used in your home, and inquire whether pet-safe formulas, such as electrical currents or liquid nitrogen, are available. If your house must be treated chemically, arrange to board your bird at your avian veterinarian's office or with a friend before, during, and after the fumigation to ensure that no harm comes to your bird. Make sure your house is aired out completely before bringing your bird home, too.

If you have other pets in the home who require flea treatments, consider using pyrethrin-based products in your home. These natural flea killers are derived from chrysanthemums and, although they aren't as long-lasting as synthetic substitutes, they do knock down fleas quickly and are safer in the long run for your pets and you. Or you can treat your dog's or cat's sleeping area with diatomaceous earth, which is the crushed shells of primitive one-celled algae. This dust kills fleas by mechanical means, which means that fleas will never develop a resistance to it as they could with chemical products.

Other Pets

Other pets can be harmful to your conure's health, too. A curious cat could claw or bite your bird, a dog could step on him accidentally or bite him, or another larger bird could break his leg or rip off his upper mandible with his beak. If your conure tangles with another pet in your home, contact your avian veterinarian immediately because emergency treatment (for bacterial infection from a puncture wound or shock from being stepped on or suffering a broken bone) may be required to save your conure's life.

Chapter 6. Everyday Care

A conure requires care every day to ensure his health and well-being. Birds are happiest when they are secure and comfortable in a safe environment. You can help your conure feel more secure by establishing a daily routine and performing the same tasks at around the same time every day. This way, your conure knows him needs will be met by the people he considers to be his family.

Here are some of the things I do every single day for my conure:

•I observe my bird for any changes in his behavior or routine. Always report any changes to your avian veterinarian immediately, if there are any.

• I always give my conure fresh food and remove old food. Make a point of washing the food dish thoroughly with detergent and water. Rinse thoroughly and allow the dish to air dry.

• I remove the water dish and replace it with a clean dish full of fresh water. Then wash the soiled dish thoroughly with detergent and water.

• I also change the paper in the cage tray.

• I also let the bird out of his cage for supervised playtime.

Finally, I always cover my bird's cage at about the same time every night to let him know it's bedtime. When you cover the cage, you'll probably hear your bird rustling around for a bit, perhaps getting a drink of water or the last mouthful of seeds before settling in for the night. Keep in mind that your conure will require ten to twelve hours of sleep a day, but you can expect that he will take naps during the day to supplement his nightly snooze.

Be Alert to Health Problems

Although it may seem a bit unpleasant to discuss, bird's droppings require daily monitoring because they can tell a lot about their general health. Conures will produce tubular droppings that appear green in the center with a whitish edge.

These droppings are usually composed of equal amounts of fecal material (the green edge), urine (the clear liquid portion), and urates (the white or cream- colored center). A healthy conure eliminates between twenty-five and fifty times a day, although a bird may go more or less often.

Texture and consistency, along with frequency or lack of droppings, can let you know how your pet is feeling. For instance, if a bird eats a lot of fruits and vegetables, his droppings are looser and more watery than a bird who primarily eats seeds. But watery droppings can also indicate illness, such as diabetes or kidney problems, which causes a bird to drink more water than usual.

The color of the droppings can also be an indication of health. Birds who have psittacosis typically have bright lime-green droppings, while healthy birds have avocado or darker green and white droppings. Birds with liver problems may produce droppings that are yellowish or reddish, while birds who have internal bleeding will produce dark, tarry droppings.

A color change doesn't necessarily indicate poor health. For example, birds who eat pelleted diets tend to have darker droppings than their seed-eating companions, and parrots who have gorged on a particular fresh food soon have droppings with that characteristic color. Birds who overindulge on beets, for instance, produce bright red droppings that can look as though the bird has suffered some serious internal injury. Birds who overdo it on sweet potatoes, blueberries, or raspberries produce orange, blue, or red droppings. During pomegranate season, birds who enjoy this fruit develop violet droppings that can look alarming to an unprepared owner.

As part of my daily cage cleaning and observation of my feathered friend, I always look at his droppings carefully. Learn what is normal for your bird regarding color, consistency, and frequency and report any changes to your avian veterinarian promptly.

Seasonal Needs
Warm weather requires a little extra vigilance on my part to make sure my conure remains comfortable. To help keep my pet cool, I keep him out of direct sun, offer him lots of fresh, juicy vegetables and fruits (be sure to remove these fresh foods from the cage promptly to keep your bird from eating spoiled food), and mist him lightly with a clean spray bottle filled with plain water. Use this bottle only for misting your bird.

On a warm day, I always notice my bird sitting with his wings held away from his body, rolling his tongue, and holding his mouth open. This is how a bird cools himself off. Oversee your bird on warm days because he can overheat quickly and may suffer heat stroke, which requires veterinary

44

care. If you live in a warm climate, ask your avian veterinarian how you can protect your bird from this potentially serious problem.

Cleaning the Cage

Cage cleaning should be part of your weekly care routine. Here's how I do it. I remove my bird and all cage accessories before cleaning the cage. Then wipe off (or scrape off) old food from the cage bars and the corners of the cage.

I then place the empty cage in the shower stall and turn on the shower. Running hot water over the cage helps loosen stuck-on food and other debris. I then scrub the cage with a toothbrush or other stiff-bristled small brush to loosen anything that remains on the cage after it's been in the shower.

After all the debris has been removed, I disinfect the cage with a bird-safe spray-on disinfectant that I buy at a pet supply store. Let the disinfectant remain on the cage bars as directed by the instructions on the bottle and then rinse thoroughly to remove the disinfectant from the cage. I then dry the cage completely. While the cage is drying, I clean the perches and accessories.

I always scrape and wash the perches to keep them clean and free of debris. (Sand the perches with coarse grain sandpaper from time to time to improve traction for your pet). I also replace perches that are very chewed or cannot be cleaned.

I thereafter rotate the toys in the cage to keep my conure's environment interesting. I then discard toys that are broken, frayed, or worn to protect my bird's health.

When the cage is completely dry, I replace the accessories and put my bird back into his newly cleaned home. I then clean the play gym the same way I cleaned the cage.

Warm weather may also bring out a host of insect pests to bedevil you and your bird. Depending on where you live, you may see ants, mosquitoes, or other bugs around your bird's cage as the temperature rises. Take care to keep your bird's cage scrupulously clean to discourage any pests, and remove any fresh food promptly to keep insects out of your bird's food bowl. Finally, in cases of severe infestation, you may have to use Camicide or other bird-safe insecticides to reduce the insect population. (Remove your bird from the area of infestation before spraying). If the problem becomes severe enough to require professional exterminators, make arrangements to have your bird stay out of the house for at least twenty-four hours after spraying has taken place.

You must also pay attention to your conure's needs when the weather turns cooler. You may want to use a heavier cage cover, especially if you lower the heat in your home at night, or move the bird's cage to another location in your home that is warmer and less drafty.

Entertaining Your Conure

In addition to keeping a conure fed and clean, you must also look after his intellectual and emotional well-being. This means paying attention to my conure each and every day and giving him things to do to challenge his mental and physical abilities.

Following is a list of games that will be as amusing for you as they are for your bird. As additional entertainment, offer your conure an interesting variety of food, both in the morning and in the evening. Make your pet work for some of his food to make mealtimes mentally stimulating. Offer peas in the pod, peanuts or other nuts in the shell, or whole green beans.

In addition to playing games with your bird, give him things he can use to amuse himself.

• The shell game: This variation on the old carnival sideshow game is fun for your bird. In the avian version, you can hide a favorite treat under a nut cup or paper muffin cup and let your bird guess which shell hides the prize.

• The great escape: Offer your bird a clean, knotted-up piece of rope or vegetable-tanned leather and see how long it takes him to untie the knots. Give your bird extra points if he doesn't chew through any of the knots to untie them.

• The mechanic: Give your conure a clean nut and bolt with the nut screwed on and see how long it takes him to undo the nut. Make sure the nut and bolt are large enough that your pet won't accidentally swallow either while playing.

• Peek-a-boo: Put a beach towel loosely over your conure then let the bird work his way out from under it. Heap lavish amounts of praise on your pet for being so clever to find his way out.

• Tug-of-war: Give your bird one end of an empty paper towel roll and tug gently. Chances are your parrot won't easily let go, or if he does, he will quickly be back for more!

In addition to playing games, you should encourage your conure to learn how to entertain himself from an early age, so he does not become overly dependent on you, because this over-dependence may lead to screaming, feather picking, or other behavioral problems if the bird feels neglected.

Chapter 7. Feeding Your Conure

Conures can live to be 40 years old, but many pet birds do not live past the age of 15. In the past, when most pet conures were caught in the wild and imported, they rarely survived past the age of 10 due to their inadequate diet. Besides shortening a bird's life span, a poor diet causes some health problems, including respiratory infections, poor feather condition, flaky skin, and reproductive problems.

The good news for conure owners is that these birds are not known to be particularly fussy when it comes to food. They eat a wide variety of things and are not as shy about trying new foods as other parrot species may be.

A Balanced Diet

According to avian veterinarians, birds require vitamins A, D, E, K, B1, B2, niacin, B6, B12, pantothenic acid, biotin, folic acid, and choline to stay healthy, but they can only partially manufacture vitamin D3 and niacin in their bodies. A balanced diet can help provide the rest.

Pet birds also need trace amounts of some minerals to maintain good health. These minerals are calcium, phosphorus, sodium, chlorine, potassium, magnesium, iron, zinc, copper, sulphur, iodine, and manganese. They can be provided with a well-balanced diet and a supplemental mineral block or cuttlebone.

Ideally, my conure's diet contains about equal parts of seeds, grains, and legumes, and dark green or dark orange vegetables and fruits. You can supplement these with small amounts of well-cooked meat or eggs or dairy products. Let's look at each part of this diet in a little more detail.

Seeds, Grains, and Legumes

This portion of your bird's diet can include clean, fresh seed from your local pet supply store. Try to buy your bird seed from a store where stock turns over quickly. The dusty box on the bottom shelf isn't as nutritious for your pet as a bulk purchase of seeds from a freshly filled bin. When you bring the seeds home, refrigerate them to keep them from becoming infested with bugs.

To ensure your bird is receiving the proper nutrients from his diet, you need to know whether the seed you're serving is fresh. One way to do this is to try sprouting some of the seeds. Sprouted seeds can also tempt a finicky eater to broaden his diet.

To sprout seeds, you will need to soak them overnight in lukewarm water. Drain the water off and let the seeds sit in a closed cupboard or other out-of-the-way place for twenty-four hours. Rinse the sprouted seeds thoroughly before offering them to your bird. If the seeds don't sprout, they aren't fresh, and you'll need to find another source for your bird's food.

Be sure, too, that your pet has an adequate supply of seeds in his dish at all times. Some conures drop the empty seed hulls back into their dishes. This seemingly full dish can lead to a very hungry conure if you aren't observant enough to check the dish carefully. Rather than just looking in the dish while it's in the cage, I suggest that you take the dish out and inspect it over the trash can so you can empty the seed hulls and refill the dish easily.

Other items in the bread group that you can offer your pet include unsweetened breakfast cereals, whole-wheat bread, cooked beans, cooked rice, and pasta. Offer a few flakes of cereal at a time, serve small bread cubes, and conure-size portions of rice, beans, or pasta.

One foodstuff that is quite popular with many conures is mung beans. Ask for them at your pet supply store and, if you're unsuccessful, check with a health food store or an Asian grocery in your area.

Fruits and Vegetables
Dark green or dark orange vegetables and fruits contain vitamin A, an important part of a bird's diet that is missing from seeds, grains, and legumes. This vitamin helps fight off infection and keeps a bird's eyes, mouth, and respiratory system healthy. Some vitamin A-rich foods are carrots, yams, sweet potatoes, broccoli, dried red peppers, and dandelion greens.

You may be wondering whether to offer frozen or canned vegetables and fruits to your bird. Some birds will eat them, while others turn their beaks up at the somewhat mushy texture of these defrosted foodstuffs. The high sodium content in some canned foods may make them unhealthy for your conure. Frozen and canned foods will do in an emergency, but I would offer only fresh foods as a regular part of his diet.

Protein
Along with small portions of well-cooked meat, you can also offer your bird bits of tofu, water-packed tuna, fully cooked scrambled eggs, cottage cheese, unsweetened yogurt, or low-fat cheese. Don't overdo the dairy

49

products, though, because a bird's digestive system lacks the enzyme lactase, which means he is unable to process dairy foods fully.

Introduce young conures to healthy human food early so that they learn to appreciate a varied diet. Some adult birds cling tenaciously to seed-only diets, which aren't healthy for them. Offer adult birds fresh foods, too, in the hope that they may try something new.

Whatever fresh foods you offer your pet, be sure to remove food from the cage promptly to prevent spoiling and to help keep your bird healthy. Ideally, you should change the food in your bird's cage every two to four hours (about every thirty minutes in warm weather), so a conure should be all right with a tray of food to pick through in the morning, another to select from during the afternoon, and a third fresh salad to nibble on for dinner.

Supplements

You may be concerned about whether your bird is receiving enough vitamins and minerals in his diet. If your conure's diet is mostly seeds and fresh foods, you may want to sprinkle a good-quality vitamin and mineral powder onto the fresh foods, where it has the best chance of sticking to the food and being eaten.

Vitamin-enriched seed diets may provide some supplementation, but some of them add the vitamins and minerals to the seed hulls, which your pet will discard while he's eating. Don't add vitamin and mineral supplements to your bird's water dish, because they can act as a growth medium for bacteria. They may also cause the water to taste different, which might discourage your bird from drinking.

Water

You will need to provide your conure with fresh, clean water twice a day to maintain his good health. You may want to give your birds water in a shallow dish, or you may find that a water bottle does the trick. If you are considering a water bottle, be aware that some clever conures have been known to stuff a seed into the drinking tube, which lets all the water drain out of the bottle. This creates a thirsty bird and a soggy cage, neither of which is ideal.

Off Limits

Now that we've looked at foods that are good for your bird let's look briefly at those that aren't. Among those foods considered harmful to pet birds are alcohol, rhubarb, avocado (the skin and the area around the pit

50

can be toxic), as well as highly salted, sweetened, and fatty foods. You also want to avoid giving your bird seeds or pits from apples, apricots, cherries, peaches, pears, and plums, because they can be harmful.

Chocolate can kill your conure, so resist the temptation to share this snack with him. It contains the chemical theobromine, which birds cannot digest as people can.

Let common sense be your guide in choosing which foods can be offered to your bird: If it's healthy for you, it's probably okay to share. However, remember to reduce the size of the portion.

While sharing healthy human food with your bird is completely acceptable, sharing something that you've already taken a bite of is not. Human saliva has bacteria in it that is perfectly normal for humans but that are potentially toxic to birds, so please don't share partially eaten food with your pet. For your bird's health and your peace of mind, give him a portion of his own, on his own plate.

The Pelleted Diet Option

Pelleted diets are created by mixing as many as forty different nutrients into a mash and then forcing the hot mixture through a machine to form various shapes. Some pelleted diets have colors, and flavors added, while others are fairly plain.

These formulated diets provide balanced nutrition for your pet bird in an easy-to-serve form that reduces the amount of wasted food and eliminates the chance for a bird to pick through a smorgasbord of healthy foods to find his favorites and reject the foods he isn't particularly fond of. Some conures accept pelleted diets quickly, while others require some persuading.

To convert your pet to a pelleted diet, offer pellets alongside or mixed in with his current diet. Once you see that your bird is eating the pellets, begin to gradually increase the number of pellets you offer at mealtime while decreasing the amount of other food you serve. Within a couple of weeks, your bird should be eating his pellets with gusto!

Although most conures aren't shy about trying new foods, yours may be hesitant to accept pellets. If your conure seems a bit finicky about trying pellets, another bird in the house may show your conure how yummy pellets can be, or you may have to act as if you are enjoying the pellets as a snack in front of your pet. Play up your apparent enjoyment of this new food because it will pique your bird's curiosity and make the pellets seem exceedingly interesting.

The advantage to a pelleted diet is that your bird can't just pick out his favorite foods and leave the rest untouched.

Whatever you do, don't starve your bird into trying a new food. Offer new foods along with familiar favorites. This will ensure that your bird is eating and will also encourage him to try new foods. Don't be discouraged if your conure doesn't dive right into a new food. Be patient, keep offering new foods to your bird, and praise him enthusiastically when he samples something new!

Chapter 8. Grooming a Conure

Although birds preen and maintain their feathers on their own, your conure needs your help with several grooming chores. First, he should be able to bathe regularly, and you need to arrange his bath for him. He will also need to have his nails and flight feathers trimmed periodically to ensure his safety.

Although you might think your Conure's beak also needs trimming, the fact is that a healthy bird supplied with enough chew toys seems to do a remarkable job of keeping his beak trimmed. If your bird's beak becomes overgrown, please consult your avian veterinarian. A parrot's beak contains a surprising number of blood vessels, so beak trimming is best left to the experts. Also, a suddenly overgrown beak may indicate that your bird is suffering from liver damage, a virus, or scaly mites, all of which require veterinary care.

Conures Love Water

As a general rule, conures are true water babies and can't get enough of being wet! If they can't bathe in their water bowl, a special bathing dish, or under the faucet in the kitchen or bathroom sink, they may take a quick roll through their food bowl, especially if there are a lot of damp, dark green, leafy vegetables in it. You may notice that your bird is particularly motivated to bathe when you vacuum the room in which he lives. Experts think the sound of a vacuum cleaner reminds conures of some distant time when they lived in the jungles and thunderstorms were brewing.

Regardless of how you provide the bird bath, be sure to set bath time early enough in the day so your pet's feathers can dry before bedtime, or you can use a blow dryer set on low to help the process along. Unless your conure has gotten himself into oil, paint, wax, or some other substance that elbow grease alone won't remove and that could harm his feathers, he will not require soap as part of his bath. Under customary conditions, soaps and detergents can damage a bird's feathers by removing beneficial oils, so hold the shampoo during your conure's normal clean-up routine!

Nail Clipping

Conures need to have their nails clipped occasionally to prevent the nails from catching on toys or perches and injuring the bird. You need to remove only tiny portions of the nail to keep your conure's claws trimmed. A good guideline to follow is to only remove the hook on each nail and to do this in the smallest increments possible.

You may find that you have better luck filing your bird's nails with an emery board than with conventional nail clippers. Whatever method you choose, stop trimming well before you reach the quick (the bundle of nerves and blood vessels that runs through the center of the nail), which is difficult to see in a conure's black toenails. If you do happen to cut the nail short enough to make it bleed, apply cornstarch or flour, followed by direct pressure, to stop the bleeding.

Wing Trimming

The goal of a properly done wing trim is to prevent your bird from flying away or flying into a window, mirror, or wall while he's out of his cage. An added benefit of trimming your pet's wings is that his inability to fly well will make him more dependent on you for transportation, which should make him easier to handle.

However, the bird still needs enough wing feathers so that he can glide safely to the ground if he is startled and takes flight from his cage top or play gym. Because proper wing trimming is a delicate balance, you may want to enlist the help of your avian veterinarian, at least the first time. Wing trimming is a task that must be done carefully to avoid injuring your pet, so take your time if you're doing it yourself. Please do not just take up the largest pair of kitchen shears you own and start snipping away. I have heard stories from avian veterinarians about birds whose owners cut off their birds' wing tips (down to the bone) in this manner.

Be particularly alert after a molt, because your bird will have a whole new crop of flight feathers that need attention. You'll be able to tell when your bird is due for a trim when he starts becoming bolder in his flying attempts. Right after a wing trim, a conure tries to fly and finds he's unsuccessful in the attempt. He will keep trying, though, and may surprise you one day with a fairly good glide across his cage or off his play-gym. If this happens, get the scissors and trim those wings immediately. If you don't, the section at the end of this chapter on finding lost birds may have more meaning for you.

Tail Feathers

Under normal circumstances, your conure's tail feathers do not need trimming. Some conures may thrash their tail feathers in the course of their normal activities, and you may feel better about your bird's appearance if you trim the scruffy-looking feathers. However, if your bird's tail feathers are often damaged or ratty-looking, your conure's cage may be too small for him to move about easily and comfortably. Remember that your pet's cage should be spacious enough for him to move around easily, extend his wings fully, and not have the tip of his tail feathers touch the floor of the cage. If your bird's cage fails these simple tests, get a larger cage for your conure and use the smaller cage as a travel cage or as a temporary home when you're cleaning the main cage.

Wing Trimming Step by Step

The first step in trimming your conure's wing feathers is to assemble all the things you will need and find a quiet, well-lit place to groom your pet before you catch and trim him. I encourage you to groom your pet in a quiet, well-lit place because grooming excites some birds and causes them to become unsettled.

Your grooming tools will include:

• Washcloth or small towel to wrap your conure in
• Small, sharp scissors to do the actual trimming
• Needle-nosed pliers (to pull out any blood feathers you may cut accidentally)
• Flour or corn-starch (not styptic powder) to stop the bleeding in case a blood feather is cut
• Nail trimmers (while you have your bird wrapped in the towel, you might as well do his nails, too)

Once you've assembled your supplies and found a quiet grooming location, drape the towel over your hand and catch your conure with your toweled hand. Gently grab your bird by the back of his head and neck (never compress the chest) and wrap him in the towel—firmly enough to hold him but not too tight!

Hold your bird's head securely through the towel with your thumb and index finger. (Having the bird's head covered by the towel will calm him and will give him something to chew on while you clip his wings). Lay the bird on his back, being careful not to constrict or compress his chest (remember, birds have no diaphragms to help them breathe), and spread his wing out carefully. You will see an upper row of short feathers, called the covert feathers, and a lower row of long feathers, which are the flight feathers.

Look for new flight feathers that are still growing in, also called blood feathers. These can be identified by their waxy, tight look (new feathers in their feather sheaths resemble the end of a shoelace) and their dark centers or quills—the dark color is caused by the blood supply to the new feather. Never trim a blood feather.

If your bird has some blood feathers, you may want to put off trimming his wings for a few days, because older, fully grown feathers act as a cushion to protect those just coming in from life's hard knocks. If your bird has only one or two blood feathers, you can trim the full-grown feathers accordingly.

To trim your bird's feathers, separate each one away from the other flight feathers and cut it individually (remember, the goal is to have a well-trimmed bird who is still able to glide a bit if he needs to). Start from the tip of the wing when you trim and clip just five to eight feathers in. Use the primary covert feathers (the set of feathers above the primary flight feathers) as a guideline as to how short you should trim—trim the flight feathers, so they are just a tiny bit longer than the coverts.

Be sure to trim an equal number of feathers from each wing. Although some people think that a bird needs only one trimmed wing, this is incorrect and could actually harm a bird who tries to fly with one trimmed and one untrimmed wing. Think of how off balance that would make you feel; your conure is no different.

Now that you've successfully trimmed your bird's wing feathers congratulate yourself. You've just taken a great step toward keeping your conure safe. Now you must remember to check your conures' wing feathers and re-trim them periodically (about four times a year is a minimum).

Blood Feather First Aid

If you do happen to cut a blood feather, remain calm. You must remove it and stop the bleeding to ensure that your bird doesn't bleed to death, and panicking will do neither of you any good.

To remove a blood feather, take a pair of needle-nosed pliers and grasp the broken feather's shaft as close to the skin of the wing as you can. With one steady motion, pull the feather out completely. After you've removed the feather, put a pinch of flour or cornstarch on the feather follicle (the spot you pulled the feather out of) and apply direct pressure for a few minutes until the bleeding stops. If the bleeding doesn't stop after a few minutes of direct pressure, or if you can't remove the feather shaft, contact your avian veterinarian immediately for further instructions.

Although it may seem like you're hurting your conure by removing the broken blood feather, consider this: A broken blood feather is like an open faucet. If left in, the faucet stays open and lets the blood out. Once removed, the bird's skin generally closes up behind the feather shaft and shuts off the faucet.

Molting

At least once a year, your conure will lose his feathers. Don't be alarmed—this is a normal process called molting. Many pet birds seem to be in a perpetual molt, with feathers falling out and coming in throughout the summer.

You can consider your bird to be in molting season when you see many whole feathers in the bottom of the cage and you notice that he seems to have broken out in a rash of stubby little bumps that look like aglets (the plastic tips on the ends of your shoelaces). These bumps are the feather sheaths that help new pinfeathers break through the skin, and they are made of keratin (the same material that makes up your fingernails). The sheaths also help protect growing feathers from damage until the feather completes its growth cycle.

You may notice that your conure is a little more irritable during the molt; this is to be expected. Think about how you would feel if you suddenly had all these itchy new feathers coming in. However, your bird may actively seek out more time with you during the molt, because owners are handy to have around when a conure has an itch on the top of his head that he can't quite scratch!

Scratch these new feathers gently, because some of them may still be growing in and may be sensitive to touch. You may want to try rolling the newly forming feathers gently between your fingers to open up the feather sheaths without causing your conure too much discomfort.

Some birds may benefit from special conditioning foods during the molting. Check with your avian veterinarian to see if your bird is a candidate for these foods.

If Your Conure Flies Away

Now that we have covered wing trimming, it's as good a time as any to discuss the possibility of your bird escaping. One of the most common accidents that befalls bird owners is that a fully flighted bird (one with untrimmed wings) escapes through an open door or window. Just because your bird has never flown before or shown any interest in leaving his home—or even his cage—doesn't mean that he can't fly or that he won't become disoriented once he's outside. If you don't believe it can happen, just check the lost and found advertisements in your local newspaper for a week. Chances are many birds will turn up in the "lost" column, and few are ever found.

Why don't lost birds come home? Some fall victim to predators in the wild, while others join flocks of feral, or wild, parrots (Florida and California are particularly noted for these). Still, other lost birds end up miles away from home because they fly wildly and frantically in any direction. And the people who find them don't advertise in the same area that the birds were lost in. Finally, some people who find lost birds don't advertise that they've been found because the finders think that whoever was unlucky or uncaring enough to lose the bird in the first place doesn't deserve to have him back.

How to Catch an Escaped Bird

If, despite your best efforts, your bird escapes, you must act quickly for the best chance of recovering your pet. Here are some things to keep in mind:

• If possible, keep the bird in sight. This will make chasing him easier.
• Make an audiotape of your bird's voice (so you're ready for just such an emergency) and play it outside on a portable tape recorder to lure your bird back home.
• Place your bird's cage in an area where he is likely to see it, such as on a deck or a patio. Put lots of treats and food on the floor of the cage to tempt your pet back into his home.
• Use another caged bird to attract your conure's attention.
• Alert your avian veterinarian's office that your bird has escaped. Also, let the local humane society and other veterinary offices in your area know.
• Post fliers in your neighborhood describing your bird. Offer a reward and include your phone number.
• Don't give up hope.

Bird tracking

GPS Technology is allowing us to take better care of our pets and provide a safer environment for them both at home and on the road.

As much as we love our pets, sometimes things happen, and one of them escapes. It is heartbreaking to see a sign attached to a utility pole bearing a picture of a lost conure. Sure, we kept their tags up to date, and perhaps they even have a chip that can be read by an animal shelter, but both of these safety measures depend on someone else finding your pet bird and following the process to return him to you. In the interim, what do you do?

Signs and pictures on utility poles aside, there is a better way to find your favorite escape artist.

Let's stop worrying and add some cutting edge technology to our pet's collar that will help us find our pet before someone else does. These GPS devices are effective, and can be accurate to within 18 inches (which is great for finding your conure at night tucked under a parked car).

Garmin, RoamEO, and PetSafe are three brands that are now making GPS collars for pet use. With this current move toward providing GPS systems for pet owners in general, we have an opportunity to better track and find our wayward pets. These types of collars are available for birds such as conures and also come with a hand-held tracking unit.

These Garmin GPS' or any other brands are a must for anyone who travels with their bird for instance. In addition to the pet collar, there is a GPS system which makes finding your lost conure as easy as checking your smart phone, tablet or laptop, and making your way to the little escaped bird.

Also worth mentioning, the Geo-Fencing feature allows you to draw an invisible boundary around your conure. If your conure crosses the line, you'll immediately receive an email or text to alert you. No shock treatment for your beloved bird.

Keeping Your Bird Safe

How can you prevent your bird from becoming lost? Here are some tips:

• Make sure his wings are safely trimmed at regular intervals.
• Trim both wings evenly and remember to trim them after your bird has molted.
• Make sure your bird's cage door locks securely and that his cage tray cannot losen if the cage is knocked over or dropped accidentally.
• Check your window screens to be sure they fit securely and are free from tears and holes.
• Keep all window screens, and patio doors closed when your bird is at liberty.
• Never go outside with your bird on your shoulder.

Chapter 8. Keeping Your Conure Healthy

In general, conures have a strong survival instinct, and even when ill, will continue to act normally for long periods of time. But conures, like all pets, can get sick or injured. Since birds can't describe how they are feeling, it is imperative that you understand the basics of your pet's physiology as well as the signs of illness. With preventive measures, early detection, and good care, the odds for a successful recovery are great.

Avian Anatomy

You may be surprised to find out that your conure's body is not all that different from your own body. You both have skin, a skeleton, respiratory, cardiovascular, digestive, excretory, and nervous systems, and sensory organs, although the various systems work in slightly different ways.

Skin

Your bird's skin is difficult to see, since your conure has so many feathers. If you part the feathers carefully, though, you can see thin, seemingly transparent skin and the muscles beneath it. Modified skin cells help make up your bird's beak, cere, claws, and the scales on his feet and legs.

Birds cannot perspire as mammals do because birds have no sweat glands, so they must have a way to cool themselves off. On a warm day, you may notice your bird sitting with his wings held away from his body, rolling his tongue, and holding his mouth open. This is how a bird cools himself off. Watch your bird carefully on warm days because he can overheat quickly, and he may suffer from heatstroke, which requires veterinary care. If you live in a warm climate, ask your avian veterinarian how you can protect your bird from this serious problem.

Musculoskeletal System

Next, let's look at your bird's skeleton. Did you know that some bird bones are hollow? These are lighter, making flying easier, but it also means these bones are more susceptible to breakage. For this reason, you must always handle your bird carefully! Another adaptation for flight is that the bones of a bird's wing (which correspond to our arm and hand bones) are fused for greater strength.

Birds also have air sacs in some of their bones (these are called pneumatic bones) and in certain body cavities that help lighten the bird's body and also cool him more efficiently. Parrots have ten neck vertebrae, compared to a human's seven. This makes a parrot's neck more mobile than a person's (a parrot can turn his head almost 180 degrees). This gives the parrot an advantage in spotting food or predators in the wild.

Instead, the bird's body wall expands and contracts, much like a fireplace bellows. This action brings air into the air sacs mentioned earlier as part of the skeleton. This action also moves air in and out of the lungs.

Although a bird's respiratory system is extremely efficient at exchanging gases in the system, two complete breaths are required to do the same work that a single breath does in people and other mammals. This is why you may notice that your bird seems to be breathing quite quickly.

Nervous System
Your conure's nervous system is very similar to your own. Both are made up of the brain, the spinal cord, and countless nerves throughout the body that transmit messages to and from the brain.

Cardiovascular System
Along with the respiratory system, your bird's cardiovascular system keeps oxygen and other nutrients moving throughout his body, although the circulatory path in your conure differs from yours. In your conure, blood flowing from the legs, reproductive system and lower intestines pass through the kidneys on its way back to the general circulatory system.

Like you, though, your conure has a four-chambered heart, with two atria and two ventricles. Unlike your average heart rate of 72 beats per minute, your conure's average heart rate is 340 to 600 beats per minute.

Digestive System
Your bird's body needs fuel for energy. Birds' bodies are fueled by food, which is where your bird's digestive system comes in. The digestive system provides the fuel that maintains your bird's body temperature—which is higher than yours. (The first time I bird-sat for friends, I worried about their cockatoo's seemingly hot feet).

After another bird owner told me that birds have higher temperatures than people, though, so I stopped worrying about the bird's warm feet. Your conure's digestive system begins with his beak. The size and shape of a bird's beak depend on his food-gathering needs.

Compare and contrast the sharp, pointed beak of an eagle or the elongated bill of a hummingbird with the hooked beak of your conure. Notice the underside of your bird's upper beak if you can. It has tiny ridges in it that help your conure hold and crack seeds more easily.

Parrots don't have saliva to break down and move their food, as we do. After the food leaves your bird's mouth, it travels down the esophagus, where it is moistened.

The food then travels to the crop, where it is moistened further and is passed in small increments into the bird's gizzard. Between the crop and the gizzard, food passes through the proventriculus, where digestive juices are added. Once in the gizzard, the food is broken down into even smaller pieces. The food next travels to the small intestine, where nutrients are absorbed into the bloodstream. Anything that's left over travels through the large intestine to the cloaca, which is the common chamber that collects waste before they leave the bird's body through the vent.

Along with the solid waste created by the digestive system, your conure's kidneys create urine, which is transported through ureters to the cloaca for excretion. Unlike a mammal, a bird does not have a bladder or a urethra.

Feathers

Birds are the only animals that have feathers, and they serve several purposes. Feathers help birds fly, they keep birds warm, they attract the attention of potential mates, and they help scare away predators.

Did you know that your conure has between 2,000 and 3,000 feathers on his body? These feathers grow from follicles that are arranged in rows known as pterylae. The unfeathered patches of bare skin on your conure's body are called apteria.

A feather is a remarkably designed creation. The base of the feather shaft, which fits into the bird's skin, is called the quill. It is light and hollow, but remarkably tough. The upper part of the feather shaft is called the rachis. From the rachis branch the barbs and barbules (smaller barbs) that make up most of the feather.

The barbs and barbules have small hooks on them that enable the different parts of the feather to interlock like Velcro and form the feather's vane or the web.

Feather colors are determined by combinations of pigment in the outer layer and in the interior structure of the feather. Birds have several different types of feathers on their bodies. Contour feathers are the colorful outer feathers on the body and wings. Many birds have an undercoating of down feathers that help keep them warm. Semiplume feathers are found on a bird's beak, nares (nostrils), and eyelids.

A bird's flight feathers can be classified into one of two types. Primary flight feathers are the large wing feathers that push a bird forward during flight. They are also the ones that need clipping, which we discussed in chapter 7, "Grooming Your Conure." Secondary flight feathers are found on the inner wing, and they help support the bird in flight. Primary and secondary flight feathers can operate independently. The bird's tail feathers also assist in flight by acting as a brake and a rudder.

To keep their feathers in good condition, healthy birds spend a great deal of time fluffing and preening. You may see your conure seeming to pick at the base of his tail on the top side. This is a normal behavior in which the bird removes oil from the preen gland and spreads it on his feathers. The oil helps prevent skin infections and waterproofs the feathers.

Sometimes pet birds will develop white lines or small holes on the large feathers of their wings and tails. These lines or holes are referred to as stress bars or stress lines and result from the bird being under stress as the feathers were developing. If you notice stress bars on your bird's feathers, discuss them with your avian veterinarian. Be prepared to describe anything new in your pet's routine to the veterinarian, because parrots are creatures of habit and sometimes react negatively to changes in their surroundings, diet, or daily activities.

Avian Senses

Taste
Compared to other mammals, the sense of taste is poorly developed in conures. Birds can taste, but in a limited way because they have fewer taste buds in their mouths than people do. Also, their taste buds are contained in the roofs of their mouths, (not in the tongue, as ours are). Experts, therefore, think a parrot's sense of taste is poorly developed.

Vision
Conures have a well-developed sense of sight. Birds see detail, and they can discern colors. Be aware of this when selecting cage accessories for your pet, because some birds react to changes in the color of their food dishes. Some seem excited by a different colored bowl, while others act fearful of the new item.

Because their eyes are located on the sides of their heads, most pet birds rely on monocular vision, which means they use each eye independent of the other. If a bird wants to study an object, you will see him tilt his head to one side and examine the object with just one eye.

Like cats and dogs, birds have a third eyelid called the nictitating membrane that you will sometimes see flick briefly across your conure's eye. The purpose of this membrane is to keep the eyeball moist and clean. If you see your conure's nictitating membrane for more than a brief second, contact your avian veterinarian for an evaluation.

You have probably noticed that your bird lacks eyelashes. In their place are small feathers called semiplumes that help keep dirt and dust out of the bird's eyeball.

Hearing

You may be wondering where your conure's ears are. Look carefully under the feathers behind and below each eye to find them. The ears are somewhat large holes in the sides of your bird's head. Conures have the same ability to distinguish sound waves and determine the location of the sound as people do, but birds seem to be less sensitive to higher and lower pitches than their owners.

Your conure's ears are behind and below each eye. You can see a very slight break in the feathers on this bird.

Smell

How does your conure's sense of smell compare to your own? Birds seem to have a poorly developed sense of smell because smells often dissipate quickly in the air (where flying birds spend the majority of their time).

Touch

The final sense we relate to, touch, is well-developed in parrots. Parrots use their feet and their mouths to touch their surroundings (young birds, particularly, seem to "mouth" everything they can get their beaks on), to play, and to determine what is safe to perch on or chew on or eat.

Along with their tactile uses, a parrot's feet also have an unusual design compared to other caged birds. Unlike a finch, for example, which has three toes pointing forward and one back, two of the conure's toes point forward and two point backward in an arrangement called zygodactyl. This enables a parrot to climb up, down, and around trees easily. Some larger parrots also use their feet to hold food or to play with toys.

Visiting the Veterinarian

With good care, a conure can live up to 40 years, although the average life span of a pet conure is about 15 years. One of the reasons conures don't live longer is that their owners may be reluctant to take their pets to the veterinarian. Some people don't want to pay veterinary bills for relatively "inexpensive" birds.

Choosing an Avian Veterinarian

As a caring owner, you want your bird to have good care and the best chance to live a long, healthy life. To that end, you will need to find a veterinarian who understands the special medical needs of birds and one with whom you can establish a good working relationship. The best time to do this is when you first bring your conure home from the breeder or the pet store. If possible, arrange to visit your veterinarian's office on your way home from the breeder or store. This is particularly important if you have other birds at home because you don't want to endanger the health of your existing flock or your new pet.

If you don't know an avian veterinarian in your area, ask the person from whom you bought your conure where they take their birds. (Breeders and bird stores usually have avian veterinarians on whom they depend). Talk to other bird owners you know and find out who they take their pets to, or call bird clubs in your area for referrals.

If you have no bird-owning friends or can't locate a bird club, your next best bet is the Yellow Pages. Read the advertisements for veterinarians carefully and try to find one who specializes in birds. Many veterinarians who have an interest in treating birds will join the Association of Avian Veterinarians and advertise themselves as members of this organization. Some veterinarians have taken and passed a special examination that entitles them to call themselves avian specialists.

Once you've received your recommendations or found likely candidates in the telephone book, start calling the veterinary offices. Ask the receptionist how many birds the doctor sees in a week or month, how much an office visit costs, and what payment options are available (cash, credit card, check, or time payments). You can also inquire whether the doctor keeps birds as pets.

If you like the answers you receive from the receptionist, make an appointment for your conure to be evaluated. (If you don't, of course, move on to the next name on your list). Make a list of any questions you want to ask the doctor regarding your bird's diet, how often your bird's wings and nails should be clipped, how often you should bring the bird in for an examination, and anything else you feel you need to know.

Plan to arrive a little early for your first appointment because you will be asked to fill out a patient information form. This form will ask you for your bird's name, his age and sex, the length of time you have owned him, your name, address, and telephone number, your preferred method of paying for veterinary services, how you heard about the veterinary office, and the name and address of a friend the veterinary office can contact in case of emergency. The form may also ask you to express your opinion on the amount of money you would spend on your pet in an emergency, because this can help the doctor know what kind of treatment to recommend in such instances.

What the Veterinarian May Ask You
Do not be afraid to ask your avian veterinarians questions. Avian vets have devoted a lot of time, energy, and effort to studying birds, so put this resource to use whenever you can. You may also be asked some questions by the veterinarian. These may include:

• Why is the bird here today?
• What is the bird's normal activity level?
• How is the bird's appetite?
• What does the bird's normal diet consist of?
• Have you noticed a change in the bird's appearance lately?

Be sure to explain any changes in as much detail as you can, because changes in your bird's normal behavior can indicate illness.

The Physical Exam
After the question-and-answer session with you, the exam will begin. Your veterinarian will probably take his or her first look at your conure while he is still in his cage or carrier. The veterinarian does this to give the bird a chance to become accustomed to his surroundings, rather than reaching in and grabbing your pet.

While the veterinarian is talking to you, he or she will check the bird's feather condition, his overall appearance, posture, and perching ability.

Next, the doctor will drape a towel over his or her hand and gently catch your conure and remove him from his carrier or cage. When the bird is out of his carrier, the doctor will look him over carefully. He or she will note the condition of your pet's eyes, his beak, and his nares. He or she will weigh your bird in a device that looks like a metal colander balanced on a scale, and the doctor will feel, or palpate, your bird's body, wings, legs, and feet for any abnormalities. He or she will also examine the bird's feathers.

Common Avian Veterinary Tests

After your veterinarian has completed your conure's physical examination, he or she may recommend further tests. These can include:

• Blood workups help a doctor determine whether your bird has a specific disease. Blood tests can be further broken down into a complete blood count, which determines how many platelets, red and white blood cells your bird has (this information can help diagnose infections or anemia), and a blood chemistry profile, which helps a veterinarian analyze how your bird's body processes enzymes, electrolytes, and other chemicals.
• X-rays enable a veterinarian to study the size and shape of a bird's internal organs and the structure of his bones. X-rays also help doctors find foreign bodies in a bird's system.
• Microbiological exams help a veterinarian determine whether any unusual organisms (bacteria, fungi, or yeast) are growing inside your bird's body.
• Fecal analysis studies a small sample of your bird's droppings to determine whether he has internal parasites or a bacterial or yeast infection.

Follow-Up Health Care

Once the examination is concluded, and you've had a chance to discuss any questions you have with your veterinarian, the doctor will probably recommend a follow-up examination schedule for your pet. Most healthy birds visit the veterinarian annually, but some need to go more frequently.

To help your veterinarian and to keep your pet from suffering long-term health risks, keep a close eye on his daily activities and appearance. If something suddenly changes in the way your bird looks or acts, contact your veterinarian immediately. Birds naturally hide signs of illness to protect them from predators, so by the time a bird looks or acts sick, he may already be dangerously ill.

Conure Health Concerns

Conures are prone to feather picking, papillomas, and psittacine beak and feather disease syndrome (PBFDS). Conures fed seed-only diets can also develop a vitamin A deficiency and other nutritional disorders.

When conures were being imported in large numbers, some of them developed a condition called conure bleeding syndrome, which I will discuss briefly in the following section, although it does not appear with the frequency it did at the height of importation.

Conure Bleeding Syndrome

Conure bleeding syndrome has been documented in blue-crowns, peach-fronts, half-moons, and Patagonians. Affected birds suffer episodes of internal bleeding that eventually kill them. These birds will have nosebleeds, difficulty breathing, weakness, diarrhea, and excessive urination. The cause is unknown, but a lack of vitamin K, calcium, and other minerals in a bird's diet may contribute to conure bleeding syndrome. Other veterinary experts believe a virus causes the condition.

Papillomas

Papillomas are benign tumors that can appear almost anywhere on a bird's skin, including his foot, leg, eyelid, or preen gland. These tumors, which are caused by a virus, can appear as small, crusty lesions, or they may be raised growths that have a bumpy texture or small projections. If a bird has a papilloma on his cloaca, the bird may appear to have a wet raspberry coming out of his vent.

Many papillomas can be left untreated without harm to the bird, but some must be removed by an avian veterinarian because a bird can pick at the growth and cause it to bleed.

Signs of Illness

To help your veterinarian and to protect your pet from long-term health problems, keep a close eye on his daily activities and appearance. If something suddenly changes in the way your bird looks or acts, contact your veterinarian immediately. Birds naturally hide signs of illness to protect themselves from predators, so by the time a bird looks or acts sick, he may already be dangerously ill.

Some signs of illness include

• A fluffed-up appearance
• Loss of appetite
• Sleeping all the time
• A change in the appearance or number of droppings
• Weight loss
• Listlessness
• Drooping wings

• Lameness
• Partially eaten food stuck to the face or food has been regurgitated onto the cage floor
• Labored breathing, with or without tail bobbing
• Runny eyes or nose
• Stops whistling, talking, or singing

If your bird shows any of these signs, please contact your veterinarian's office immediately.

Psittacine Beak and Feather Disease Syndrome

PBFDS is a virus that has been reported in more than forty species of parrots, including conures. PBFDS causes a bird's feathers to become pinched or clubbed in appearance. Other symptoms include beak fractures and mouth ulcers. This highly contagious, fatal disease is most common in birds under three years of age, and there is no cure at present.

Feather Picking

Conure owners, particularly those who own nandays and suns, need to be alert for feather picking. Don't confuse picking with normal preening. Birds who pick their feathers pluck them right out. You will see feathers on the floor of the cage and scruffy or even bald spots on your bird. Once feather picking begins, it may be difficult to get a bird to stop. Although it looks painful to us, some birds find the routine of pulling out their feathers emotionally soothing.

Conures who suddenly begin picking their feathers, especially those under the wings, may have an intestinal parasite called giardia. If you notice that your bird suddenly starts pulling her feathers out, contact your avian veterinarian for a feather evaluation. Other causes to consider include poor diet, low humidity, infrequent baths, and lack of access to regular periods of light.

Psychological causes for feather picking can include boredom, insecurity, breeding frustrations, nervousness, and stress. Stress in a bird's life can result from something as simple as rearranging the living room furniture or as complex as bringing a new child or pet into the home.

I don't have a magic solution to offer, except to ask that you have your bird evaluated by your avian veterinarian if he starts to pick. If the cause isn't physical, please be patient with your feather-picking parrot as you try to distract him away from his feathers.

Conure First Aid

Sometimes your pet will get himself into a situation that will require quick thinking and even quicker action on your part to help save him from serious injury or death.

Here are some basic first-aid techniques that may prove useful in these situations. Before we get into the specific techniques, though, make sure you have your bird owner's first aid kit.

Here are some urgent medical situations bird owners are likely to encounter, the reason they are medical emergencies, the signs and symptoms your bird might show, and what you should do for your bird.

What to Do in an Emergency
If your bird requires urgent care, keep the following in mind:
Stay as calm as possible.
Stop any bleeding.
Keep the bird warm.
Keep the bird calm and quiet.
Call your veterinarian's office for additional instructions.
Describe what has happened to your bird.
Listen carefully to any instructions you receive.
Take your bird to the veterinarian's office or veterinary urgent care clinic as soon as possible.

Animal Bites

It's an emergency because: Infections can develop from bacteria on the biting animal's teeth and claws. Also, a bird's internal organs can be damaged by the bite.

Signs: Sometimes the bite marks can be seen, but often the bird shows few, if any, signs of injury.
What to do: Call your veterinarian's office and transport the bird there immediately. Treatment for shock and antibiotics are often the steps veterinarians take to save birds who have been bitten.

Beak Injury

It's an emergency because: A bird needs both his upper and lower beak (also called the upper and lower mandible) to eat and preen properly. Infections can also set in rather quickly if a beak is fractured or punctured.
Signs: The bird is bleeding from his beak. This often occurs after the bird flies into a windowpane or a mirror, or if he has a run-in with a ceiling fan.

The bird may also have cracked or damaged his beak, and portions of the beak may be missing.

What to do: Control the bleeding (see the following section), keep the bird calm and quiet, and contact your avian veterinarian's office.

Your Conure's First Aid Kit

Assemble a bird owner's first aid kit so that you will have some basic supplies on hand before your bird needs them. Here's what to include:

• Appropriate-size towels for catching and holding your bird
• Heating pad, heat lamp, or another heat source
• Pad of paper and pencil to make notes about the bird's condition
• Styptic powder, silver nitrate stick, or cornstarch to stop bleeding (use styptic powder or silver nitrate stick on beak and nails only)
• Blunt-tipped scissors
• Nail clippers and nail file
• Needle-nosed pliers to pull broken blood feathers
• Blunt-end tweezers
• Hydrogen peroxide or other disinfectant solution
• Eye irrigation solution
• Bandage materials such as gauze squares, masking tape (it doesn't stick to a bird's feathers as adhesive tape does), and gauze rolls
• Pedialyte or another energy supplement
• Eyedropper
• Small syringes without the needles to irrigate wounds or feed sick birds
• Penlight

Bleeding

It's an emergency because: A bird can withstand only about a 20 percent loss of blood volume and still recover from an injury.

Signs: With external bleeding, you will see blood on the bird, his cage, and his surroundings. In the case of internal bleeding, the bird may pass bloody droppings or bleed from his nose, mouth, or vent.

What to do: For external bleeding, apply direct pressure. If the bleeding doesn't stop with direct pressure, apply a coagulant, such as styptic powder (for nails and beaks) or cornstarch (for broken feathers and skin injuries). If the bleeding stops, observe the bird to check for more bleeding and signs of shock. Call your veterinarian's office if the bird seems weak or if he has lost a lot of blood and arrange to take the bird in for further treatment.

Broken blood feathers can result in bleeding. Blood feathers can break horizontally (across the feather) or vertically (along with the feather shaft). Horizontal breaks are more common, and they often result from a bird pulling at a blood feather or an owner accidentally cutting a blood feather while trimming a bird's wings.

In severe cases that do not respond to direct pressure, you may have to remove the feather shaft to stop the bleeding. To do this, grasp the feather shaft as close to the skin as you can with a pair of needle-nosed pliers and pull out the shaft with a swift, steady motion. Apply direct pressure to the skin after you remove the feather shaft.

Breathing Problems

It's an emergency because: Respiratory problems in pet birds can be life-threatening.
Signs: The bird wheezes or clicks while breathing, bobs his tail, breathes with an open mouth, and has discharge from his nares or swelling around his eyes.
What to do: Keep the bird warm, place him in a bathroom with a hot shower running to help him breathe more easily, and call your veterinarian's office.

Burns

It's an emergency because: Birds who are burned severely enough can go into shock and may die.
Signs: A burned bird has reddened skin and burnt or greasy feathers. The bird may also show signs of shock.
What to do: Mist the burned area with cool water. Lightly apply antibiotic cream or spray. Do not apply any oily or greasy substances, including butter. If the bird seems shock or the burn is widespread, contact your veterinarian's office immediately for further instructions.

Concussion

It's an emergency because: A concussion results from a sharp blow to the head that can cause injury to the brain.

Signs: Birds sometimes suffer concussions when they fly into mirrors or windows. They will seem stunned and may go into shock.

What to do: Keep the bird warm, prevent him from hurting himself further, and watch him carefully. Alert your veterinarian's office to the injury.

Cloacal Prolapse

It's an emergency because: The bird's lower intestines, uterus or cloaca is protruding from the bird's vent.

Signs: The bird has pink, red, brown, or black tissue protruding from her vent.

What to do: Contact your veterinarian's office for immediate care. Your veterinarian can usually reposition the organs.

Egg Binding

It's an emergency because: The egg blocks the hen's excretory system and makes it impossible for her to eliminate. Also, eggs can sometimes break inside the hen, which can lead to infection.

Signs: An egg-bound hen strains to lay eggs unsuccessfully. He becomes fluffed and lethargic, sits on the floor of her cage, may be paralyzed, and may have a swollen abdomen.

What to do: Keep her warm, because this sometimes helps her pass the egg. Put her and her cage into a warm bathroom with a hot shower running to increase the humidity, which may also help her pass the egg. If your bird doesn't improve within an hour, contact your veterinarian.

Eye Injuries

It's an emergency because: Untreated eye problems can lead to blindness.

Signs: Swollen or pasty eyelids, discharge, cloudy eyeball, and increased rubbing of the eye area.

What to do: Scrutinize the eye for foreign bodies. Then contact your veterinarian for instructions.

Fractures

It's an emergency because: A fracture can cause a bird to go into shock. Depending on the type of fracture, infections can also set in.

Signs: Birds most often break bones in their legs, so be on the lookout for a bird who is holding one leg at an odd angle or who isn't putting weight on one leg. Sudden swelling of a leg or wing, or a droopy wing can also indicate fractures.

What to do: Confine the bird to his cage or a small carrier. Don't handle him unnecessarily. Keep him warm and contact your veterinarian.

Frostbite

It's an emergency because: A bird could lose toes or feet to frostbite. He could also go into shock and die.

Signs: The frostbitten area is very cold and dry to the touch and is pale in color.

What to do: Warm up the damaged tissue gradually in a circulating warm (not hot) water bath. Keep the bird warm and contact your veterinarian's office for further instructions.

Inhaled or Eaten Foreign Object

It's an emergency because: Birds can develop serious respiratory or digestive problems from foreign objects in their bodies.

Signs: In the case of inhaled items, symptoms include wheezing and other respiratory problems. In the case of consumed objects, you might have seen your conure playing with a small item that suddenly cannot be found.

What to do: If you suspect that your bird has inhaled or eaten something he shouldn't, contact your veterinarian's office immediately.

Lead Poisoning

It's an emergency because: Birds can die from lead poisoning.

Signs: A bird with lead poisoning may act depressed or weak. He may be blind, or he may walk in circles at the bottom of his cage. He may regurgitate or pass droppings that resemble tomato juice.

What to do: Contact your avian veterinarian immediately. Lead poisoning requires a quick start to treatment, and the treatment may require several days or weeks to complete successfully.

Overheating

It's an emergency because: High body temperatures can kill a bird.

Signs: An overheated bird will try to make himself thin. He will hold his wings away from his body, open his mouth, and roll his tongue in an attempt to cool himself. Birds don't have sweat glands, so they must try to cool their bodies by exposing as much of their skin's surface as they can to moving air.

What to do: Cool the bird off by putting him in front of a fan (make sure the blades are screened so the bird doesn't injure himself further), by spraying him with cool water, or by having him stand in a bowl of cool water. Let the bird drink cool water if he can (if he can't, offer him cool water with an eyedropper) and contact your veterinarian.

Poisoning

It's an emergency because: Poisons can kill a bird quickly.

Signs: Poisoned birds may suddenly regurgitate, have diarrhea or bloody droppings, and have redness or burns around their mouths. They may also go into convulsions, become paralyzed, or go into shock.

What to do: Put the poison out of your bird's reach. Contact your veterinarian for further instructions. Be prepared to take the poison with you to the vet's office in case he or he needs to contact a poison control center for further information.

Seizures

It's an emergency because: Seizures can indicate some serious conditions, including lead poisoning, infections, nutritional deficiency, heat stroke, and epilepsy.

Signs: The bird goes into a seizure that lasts from a few seconds to a minute. Afterward, he seems dazed and may stay on the cage floor for several hours. He may also appear unsteady and won't perch.

What to do: Keep the bird from hurting himself by removing everything you can from his cage. Cover the bird's cage with a towel and darken the room to reduce the bird's stress level. Contact your veterinarian's office immediately for further instructions.

Shock

It's an emergency because: Shock occurs when the bird's circulatory system cannot move the blood supply around the bird's body. This is a serious condition that can lead to death if left untreated.

Signs: Shocked birds may act depressed, breathe rapidly, and have a fluffed appearance. If your bird displays these signs in conjunction with a recent accident, suspect shock and take appropriate action.

What to do: Keep your bird warm, cover his cage, and transport him to your veterinarian's office as soon as possible.

Medicating Your Conure

Most bird owners are faced with the prospect of medicating their pets at some point in the birds' lives, and many are not sure whether they can complete the task without hurting their pets. If you have to medicate your pet, your avian veterinarian or veterinary technician should explain the process to you. In the course of the explanation, you should find out how you will be administering the medication, how much of the drug you will be giving your bird, how often the bird needs the medication, and how long the entire course of treatment will last.

This is a safe way to restrain your bird. Make sure not too put much pressure on his breast.

If you find (as I often have) that you've forgotten one or more of these steps after you arrive home, call your vet's office for clarification to make sure your bird receives the follow-up care from you that he needs.

Let's briefly review the most common methods of administering medications to birds. I know from personal experience that all the methods I will describe here do work and are survivable by both bird and owner.

Oral Medication
This is a good route to take with birds who are small, easy to handle, or underweight. The medication is usually given with a plastic syringe, minus the needle, placed on the left side of the bird's mouth and pointed toward the right side of his throat. This route is recommended to ensure that the medication gets into the bird's digestive system and not into his lungs, where aspiration pneumonia can result.

Medicating a bird's food or offering medicated feed is another effective possibility, but medications added to a bird's water supply are often less effective because sick birds are less likely to drink water, and the medicated water can have an unusual taste that makes the bird less likely to drink it.

Injected Medication
Avian veterinarians consider this the most effective method of medicating birds.

Some injection sites—into a vein, beneath the skin, or into a bone—are used by avian veterinarians in the clinic. Bird owners are usually asked to medicate their birds intramuscularly—by injecting medication into the bird's chest muscle. This is the area of the bird's body that has the greatest muscle mass, so it is a good injection site.

Ask your avian veterinarian to demonstrate how to give a bird an injection. Once you are comfortable with the procedure, follow the veterinarian's instructions for injecting your bird. Wrap your bird securely but comfortably in a washcloth or small towel and lay him on your lap with his chest up. Hold him head securely with your thumb and index finger of one hand, and use the other to insert the syringe at about a 45-degree angle under the bird's chest feathers and into the muscle beneath.

You should remember to alternate the side you inject your bird on (say, left in the morning and right in the evening) to ensure that one side doesn't get over-injected and sore. Remain calm and talk to your bird in a soothing tone while you're administering the drugs. Before you both know it, the shot is over, and your bird is one step closer to a complete recovery!

Topical Medication

This method, which is far less stressful than injections, provides medication directly to a part of a bird's body. Uses can include medications for eye infections, dry skin on the feet or legs, and sinus problems.

Caring for Older Birds

If you've offered your conure a varied, healthy diet, taken him to the vet regularly, clipped his wings faithfully, and kept his environment clean and interesting, chances are your bird will live to old age. You may notice subtle changes in your bird's appearance and habits as he ages. He may molt more erratically and his feathers may grow in more sparsely, or he may seem to preen himself less often.

Although little is known about the nutritional requirements of older pet birds, avian veterinarians say that older pet birds should eat a highly digestible diet that enables a bird to maintain his weight while getting lower levels of proteins, phosphorus, and sodium. They also suggest that this diet contain slightly higher levels of vitamins A, E, B12, thiamin, pyridoxine, zinc, linoleic acid, and lysine, which may help birds cope with the metabolic and digestive changes that come with old age.

When Your Conure Dies

Although conures are relatively long-lived pets, eventually the wonderful relationship between bird and owner ends when the bird dies. Although no one has an easy time accepting the death of a beloved pet, children may have more difficulty with the loss than adults. To help your child cope, consider the following suggestions.

Let your child know that it's okay to feel sad about losing your conure. Encourage your child to draw pictures of the bird, make a collage using photos of your pet or pictures of conures from magazines, write stories or poems about him, or talk about your loss. Also, explain to the child that these sad feelings will pass with time. Regardless of a child's age, being honest about the loss of your bird is the best way to help all family members cope with the loss.

While helping their children cope with the death of a pet, parents need to remember that it's okay for adults to feel sad, too. Don't diminish your feelings of loss by saying "It's only a bird." Pets fill important roles in our lives and our families. Whenever we lose someone close to us, we grieve.

Although you may feel as though you never want another bird because of the pain caused by your bird's death, don't let the loss of your conure keep you from owning other birds. Although you can never replace your conure, you may find that you miss having a feathered companion around your house.

Some people want a new pet bird almost immediately after suffering a loss, while others want to wait a few weeks or months before bringing another bird home. Maybe you want another conure, or perhaps you'd like to try owning a different species. Discuss bringing home a new pet bird with your family, your avian veterinarian, and bird breeders in your area.

Chapter 9. Conure's Behavior

As a new bird owner, you're probably wondering what constitutes normal behavior for your pet and what behaviors indicate that something isn't quite right with your conure.

As you get to know your pet and as he settles into his new routine in your home, you'll soon learn exactly what behaviors are normal for your pet. It's important for you as a bird owner to learn what is normal for your conure, because your avian veterinarian will often ask for your observations during routine examinations as well as during times of illness.

Common Conure Behaviors

The following common avian behaviors are listed in alphabetical order to help you better understand your new feathered friend.

Attention-Seeking

As your conure becomes more settled in your home, don't be surprised if you hear subtle little fluffs coming from under the cage cover first thing in the morning. It's as if your bird is saying, "I hear that you're up. I'm up, too. Don't forget to uncover me and play with me!" Other attention-seeking behaviors include gently shaking toys, sneezing, and soft vocalizations.

Bathing

Conures are great bathers and love to be dunked under the water faucet (with a gentle stream of water) while sitting on your hand or to stand under a light shower in the kitchen sink. Some birds may even enjoy showering with you, and bird-size shower perches can be purchased or made if you want to try it. If nothing else is available, your conure will try to take a bath in his water bowl. Be sure your pet's bath water is lukewarm before letting your conure take a quick dip, and allow plenty of time for your bird's feathers to dry before he goes to bed to avoid chilling him.

Beak Grinding

If you hear your bird making odd little-grinding noises as he's drifting off to sleep, don't be alarmed. Beak grinding is a sign of a contented pet bird, and it's commonly heard as a bird settles in for the night.

Beak Wiping

After a meal, it's common for a conure to wipe his beak against a perch, on your sleeve (if your arm happens to be handy), or on the cage bars to clean it.

Birdie Aerobics

This is how I describe a sudden bout of stretching that all parrots seem prone to. An otherwise calm bird will suddenly grab the cage bars and stretch the wing and leg muscles on one side of his body, or he will raise both wings in imitation of an eagle. Again, this is normal behavior.

Birdnaps

Don't be surprised if you catch your conure taking a little catnap during the day. As long as you see no other indications of illness, such as a loss of appetite or a fluffed-up appearance, there is no need to worry if your pet sleeps during the day.

Biting

If your conure bites you in the presence of strangers, he is demonstrating an instinctive flock behavior that is meant to protect you. In the wild, when conures are presented with a threat (such as a stranger), they call to one another to flee and then may bite at slower-moving members of the flock to hurry them on their way.

If your bird bites you when you are alone, he may simply be testing his environment with his mouth or he may be demonstrating how well he has trained you. If you react with a lot of dramatic attention (such as speaking in a loud voice or shaking your finger at the bird), the bird will think he has stumbled onto a great game that you will play with him each time he bites you.

Finally, a biting bird may be challenging you for control of his environment. If you want to maintain control of your bird and his environment, look sternly at your pet and use the "up" command to get the bird onto your hand. This should help keep the biting episodes to a minimum.

Chewing

Chewing helps keep a pet bird's beak in top condition, and it also provides a pet parrot with a way to use up some of his excess energy. Chewing is one of a conure's most common behaviors, which means your pet will need an abundant supply of chewable toys. These can range from empty paper towel rolls to elaborate wooden toys you buy at the pet supply store. If you don't provide a conure with appropriate outlets for his chewing urges, he will find satisfaction in gnawing on your furniture or houseplants. Be sure to supervise your conure when he is out of his cage to prevent him from chewing on inappropriate and potentially harmful things in your home.

Eye Pinning
When a conure sees something that excites or interests him, you may notice that his pupils contract, expand, and contract again. This is called eye pinning. This action will be easier to see on some conures than on others because some conure species have dark irises that blend in quite well with their pupils.

Fluffing
Fluffing is often a prelude to preening or a tension releaser. If your bird fluffs up, stays fluffed, and resembles a feathered pinecone, however, contact your avian veterinarian for an appointment because fluffed feathers can be an indicator of illness.

Possessiveness
Although it doesn't happen as often with conures as with some other parrot species, a conure can become overly attached to one person in the household, especially if that person is the one who is primarily responsible for his care. Indications of a possessive conure can include biting and other threatening gestures made toward other family members, and pair bonding behavior with the chosen family member.

You can keep your conure from becoming possessive by having all members of the family spend time with your bird from the time you first bring him home. Encourage different members of the family to feed the bird and clean his cage, and make sure all family members play with the bird and socialize with him while he's out of his cage.

Preening
Preening is one of your conure's ways of keeping himself well groomed. You will notice him ruffling and straightening his feathers each day. He will also take oil from the gland at the base of his tail and spread it on the rest of his feathers, so don't be concerned if you see your conure apparently pecking or biting at his tail. Preening, combined with your assistance in bathing and nail and wing clipping, will keep your conure in top shape.

If, during molting, your bird seems to remove whole feathers, don't panic. Old, worn feathers are pushed out by incoming new ones, which makes the old feathers loose and easy to remove.

Birds preen to keep themselves well-groomed. Friendly pairs may preen each other.

Regurgitating

If you see that your bird is pinning his eyes, bobbing his head, and pumping his neck and crop muscles, he is about to regurgitate some food for you. Birds regurgitate to their mates during the breeding season and to their young while raising chicks. It is a mark of great affection, so try not to be too disgusted if your pet starts bringing up his last meal in your honor.

Resting on One Foot

Do not be alarmed if you see your conure occasionally resting on only one foot. This is normal behavior (the resting foot is often drawn up into the belly feathers). If you see your bird always using both feet to perch, please contact your avian veterinarian because this can indicate a health problem.

Screaming

Well-cared-for conures will vocalize, but birds who feel neglected and have little attention paid to them may become screamers. Once a bird becomes a screamer, it can be a difficult habit to break, particularly because the bird feels rewarded by your negative attention every time he screams. You may not regard your scolding as a reward, but at least the bird gets to see you and to hear from you as you tell him to be quiet.

Sometimes, conures and other parrots are just a little lonesome, and in need of reassurance, so they scream to see where their people are. In these cases, simply call back to your bird with "I'm here. Are you okay?" or another reassuring phrase. In many cases, the bird will quiet down quickly after hearing your voice.

At other times, birds may scream because something in the environment frightens them. In these cases, you will have to work with the bird over time to desensitize him to whatever is scary. If your bird screams at you when you wear a hat, for example, set the hat on a table far away from the bird's cage and gradually (over a period of a few days or a week) bring the hat closer to your bird's cage. Tell your bird how brave he is as the hat gets closer to the cage, and cuddle and pet him to further reward his bravery.

Still, other birds scream because they think they have to protect their home and families. This hearkens back to the wild, where parrots alert one another to danger in the area by screaming or calling. In these cases, it's a good idea to check to see that your toaster isn't smoking or there isn't a squirrel on the patio railing before disciplining your helpful watch-parrot.

Sometimes birds will scream when they are tired. In these cases, covering the cage for a few minutes does the trick. If your bird seems to be consistently tired and cranky, you may have to adjust his bedtime. Remember that birds need about twelve hours of sleep a night, and your conure may be disturbed by evening activity, such as the family watching TV or the children doing homework with a bright desk lamp on. A heavier cage cover or relocating the bird to another part of the house at bedtime should do the trick but remember not to banish your bird to some far-flung, seldom-used part of your house because this can also cause screaming if the bird feels neglected and forgotten.

Sleeping
Conures are known for two unusual behaviors while sleeping: snuggling under something to sleep, and falling asleep on their backs in their food bowls. You may find your bird napping under a corner of his cage paper (if the cage he lives in doesn't have a grille to keep the bird out of the cage tray). To keep your pet content, give your conure a washcloth, a fuzzy toy, or something else cuddly to snuggle with.

Conures sometimes fall asleep on their backs with their feet in the air. Although this position has an alarming effect on new conure owners, there's nothing wrong with your pet. This is a perfectly comfortable position for a conure to be in.

Sneezing
In pet birds, sneezes are classified as either nonproductive or productive. Nonproductive sneezes clear a bird's nares (what we think of as nostrils) and are nothing to worry about. Some birds even stick a claw into their nares to induce a sneeze from time to time. Productive sneezes, on the other hand, produce a discharge and are a cause for concern. If your bird sneezes frequently and you see a discharge from his nares or notice the area around his nares is wet, contact your avian veterinarian immediately to set up an appointment to have your bird's health checked.

Tasting/Testing Things
Birds use their beaks and mouths to explore their world in much the same way people use their hands. For example, don't be surprised if your conure reaches out to tentatively taste or bite your hand before stepping onto it for the first time. Your bird isn't biting you to be mean; he's merely

investigating his world and testing the strength of a new perch using the tools he has available.

Birds use their beaks to explore their world and will examine many objects with their mouth.

Vocalization
Many parrots vocalize around sunrise and sunset, which may be a holdover from flock behavior in the wild. The parrots in the flock call to one another to start and end their days. You may notice that your pet conure calls to you when you are out of the room. This may mean he feels lonely or he needs some reassurance from you. Tell him he's fine and that he's being a good bird, and he should settle down and begin playing or eating. If he continues to call to you, however, you may want to check on him to make sure everything is all right.

Yawning
You may notice your conure yawning from time to time or seeming to want to pop his ears by opening his mouth wide and closing it. Some bird experts would say your bird needs more oxygen in his environment and would recommend airing out your bird room (be sure all your window and door screens are secure before opening a window or a sliding glass door to let fresh air in), while other experts would tell you your pet is merely yawning or stretching his muscles. If you see no other signs of illness accompanying the yawning, such as forceful regurgitation or vomiting, you have no cause for concern.

Moving with a Conure
If moving is in your future, your first step should be to acclimate your bird to traveling in the car. Some pet birds take to this new adventure immediately, while others become so stressed out by the trip that they become carsick. Patience and persistence are usually the keys to success if your pet falls into the latter category.

To get your conure used to riding in the car, start by taking his cage (with door and cage tray well secured) out to your car and placing it inside. Make sure your car is cool before you do this because your conure can suffer heat stroke if you place him in a hot car and leave him there.

When your bird seems comfortable sitting in his cage in your car, place the cage in the back seat, secure it with a seat belt, and take your pet for a short drive, such as around the block. If your bird seems to enjoy the ride (he eats, sings, whistles, talks, and acts like nothing is wrong), then you have a willing traveller on your hands. If he seems distressed by the ride (he sits on the floor of his cage shaking, screams, or vomits), then you have a bit of work ahead.

Distressed birds often only need to be conditioned to the idea that car travel can be fun. You can do this by talking to your bird throughout the trip. Praise him for good behavior and reassure him that everything will be fine. Offer special treats and juicy fruits (grapes, apples, or citrus fruit) so that your pet will eat and will also get some moisture.

As your bird becomes accustomed to car travel, gradually increase the length of the trips. When your bird is comfortable with car rides, begin to condition him for the move by packing your car as you would on moving day. If, for example, you plan to place duffel bags near your bird's cage, put the bags and the cage in the back of the car for a practice run before you actually begin the move so your bird can adjust to the size, shape, and color of the bags. A little planning on your part will result in a well-adjusted avian traveller and a reduced stress level for you both.

Before you move, make a final appointment with your bird's veterinarian. Have the bird evaluated, and ask for a health certificate (this may come in handy when crossing state lines). Also ask for a copy of your conure's records that you can take with you, or arrange to have a copy sent to your new address, so your bird's new avian veterinarian will know your pet's history. Once you've settled in your new home, develop a rapport with an avian veterinarian in the area and schedule your conure for a new patient exam. That way, you'll know your bird came through the move with flying colors.

Traveling with Your Bird

When I worked for Bird Talk, we often heard from bird owners who wanted to take their pets on vacation and people relocating to another state or country. The advice we gave them about traveling with their bird depended on the owner and their pet.

These were some of the questions we asked:
Does the bird like new adventures?
Is there a trusted relative or friend you can leave the bird with while you are away?
Does your avian veterinarian's office offer boarding?
How long will you be gone?

Will you be visiting a foreign country?

If the owners were going on a family vacation, we usually recommended leaving the bird at home in familiar surroundings with his own food, water, and cage or in the care of a trusted friend, relative, pet sitter, or avian veterinarian. We advised this because birds are creatures of habit who like their routines and because taking birds across state lines or international boundaries is not without risk. Some species are illegal in certain states (Quaker, or monk, parakeets, for example, are believed to pose an agricultural threat to some states because of their hearty appetites), and some foreign countries have lengthy quarantine stays for pet birds. It was our professional opinion that, although it is difficult to leave your bird behind when you travel, it is better for the bird. (Of course, if you're moving, that's a different story!) Some birds are just homebodies and prefer not to travel.

If you leave your pet at home while you're away, you have several care options available. First, you can recruit the services of a trusted friend or relative, which is an inexpensive and convenient solution for many pet owners. You can return the pet-sitting favor for your friend or relative when they go out of town.

If your trusted friends and relatives live far away, you can hire a professional pet sitter (many advertise in the Yellow Pages, and some offer additional services, such as picking up mail, watering your plants, and leaving on lights and/or radios to make your home seem occupied while you're gone). If you're not sure about what to look for in a pet sitter, the National Association of Professional Pet Sitters offers the following tips.

• Look for a bonded pet sitter who carries commercial liability insurance.
• Ask for references and a written description of services and fees.
• Arrange to have the pet sitter come to your home before you leave on your trip to meet the pets and discuss what services you would like them to perform while you're away.
• During the initial interview, evaluate the sitter. Do they seem comfortable with your bird? Do they have experience caring for birds? Do they own birds?
• Ask for a written contract and discuss the availability of vet care (whether they have an existing arrangement with your veterinarian, for example). Inquire about the arrangements the sitter makes in the event of inclement weather or personal illness.
• Discuss the sitter's policy for making sure you have returned home. Should you call them to confirm your arrival, or will they call you?

If the prospect of leaving your bird with a pet sitter doesn't appeal to you, you may be able to board your bird at your avian veterinarian's office. Of course, you'll need to find out whether your vet's office offers boarding services and decide whether you want to risk your bird's health by exposing him to other birds during boarding.

Insuring your conure

As a parrot owner, you may be asking why you need to get pet insurance for your conure. With today's rising costs for veterinary care, you may just need pet insurance for your bird for a peace of mind. There are a handful of insurance companies out there that offer comprehensive policies for conures. An insurance policy for your bird can offer you a financial solution to managing your veterinary costs by reimbursing your eligible expenses for accidents, illnesses and routine preventive care, which includes office visits, lab fees, X-rays, surgeries, diagnostic testing, prescriptions, hospitalization and more.

Your conure is a member of your family and its quality of life is important to you. An insurance plan offers a financial solution to your veterinary bills so you can focus on providing your bird health rather than on the cost of healthcare. Airborne viruses and bird flu are threats that may hurt you financially if you are not well covered.

Conures are beautiful loving pets that can live long. With all the commitment and investment that you have already made on your bird, you will need it to be covered by an insurance policy because he is always vulnerable to illnesses and health risks. A good insurance plan for a conure covers major medical treatments, surgeries for accidents, minor treatments, self-mutilation, feather plucking and neoplasia surgery. And what if your conure bites someone's hand and causes injury? In our litigious society, you need to protect yourself and your bird against all possibilities.

A good insurance policy pays up to 90% of the benefit schedule or up to 90% of the veterinary bill. Premiums may cost anywhere between $15 to $20 / £12 to £15 a month depending on the coverage. You can also easily maximize your bird's coverage by adding a coverage rider. This can help pay for a routine exam, blood testing, fecal analysis, nail and wing trim and more.

Purchasing pet insurance for your conure is a good financial plan. Accidents and illnesses do happen, and you need to be covered to have peace of mind. It would be sad if you have to resort to putting your parrot to sleep if you can't afford to face the veterinary costs.

Chapter 10. Having Fun with Your Conure

Now that you've learned the basics of caring for your new conure, it's time to enjoy your pet's companionship. Try to spend time with your bird each day to make sure his emotional needs for companionship and stimulation are being met.

Remember that you and your family are substituting for your conure's flock and that your conure is a very social little bird who needs companionship regularly to feel secure and content in his surroundings.

To make spending time with your pet each day a true pleasure, it's best to train him to follow simple commands that make him easier to handle. This way, you can take your conure with you while you are doing homework, talking on the phone, or watching television.

Your bird will benefit from the time spent with you outside his cage, and you will have more time to enjoy him. Whenever your conure is out of his cage, be sure to supervise him carefully to ensure he stays safe and healthy! (See chapter 4, "Home Sweet Home," for tips on household safety).

Taming Your Conure

Taming a parrot was one of the most popular topics of discussion when I worked at Bird Talk, and the discussion continues today among avian behaviorists and their clients in bird club meetings, books and magazine articles, and on the Internet.

The first thing to teach your conure is how to step up onto your hand.

A good first step in taming your conure is getting him to be comfortable around you. To do this, give your bird a bit of warning before you approach his cage. Don't sneak up on him and try not to startle him. Call his name when you walk into the room. Try to be quiet and move slowly around your pet. Keep your hands behind you and reassure the bird that you aren't there to harm him, that everything is all right, and that he's a wonderful conure.

After your bird is comfortable having you in the same room, try placing your hand in his cage as a first step toward taking him out. Just rest your hand in the cage, on the floor, or on a perch and hold it there, for a few seconds. Don't be surprised if your bird flutters around and squawks at first at the "intruder."

Do this several times each day, leaving your hand in the cage for slightly longer each day. Within a few days, your conure won't make a fuss about your hand being in his space, and he may come over to investigate this new perch. Do not remove your hand from the bird cage the first time your conure lands on it; just let him get used to perching on your hand.

After your conure has calmly perched on your hand for several days in a row, try to take your hand out of the cage slowly with your bird on it. Some conures will take to this new adventure willingly, while others are reluctant to leave the safety and security of home. (Be sure your bird's wings are clipped, as explained in chapter 7, "Grooming Your Conure," and all doors and windows are secured before taking your bird out of his cage).

If your bird doesn't seem to like this at all, you can try an alternate taming method. Take the bird out of his cage and into a small room, such as a bathroom, that has been bird-proofed (the toilet lid is down, the shower door is closed, all windows are closed, and the bathroom hasn't been recently cleaned with any cleansers that have strong chemical odors). Sit down on the floor, place your bird in front of you, and begin gently playing with him. Don't be surprised if your bird tries to fly a few times. With clipped wings, however, he won't get very far and will give up trying after a few failed attempts.

Step Up, Step Down
Once you've calmed your conure, see whether you can make perching on your hand a game for your pet. Once he masters perching on your hand, you can teach him to step up by gently pressing your finger up and into the bird's belly. This will cause the bird to step up. As he does so, say "step up" or "up." Before long, your bird will respond to this command without much prompting.

Along with the "up" command, you may want to teach your conure the "down." command. When you put the bird down on his cage or play gym, simply say "down" as he steps off your hand. These two simple commands give you a great deal of control over your bird because you can say "up" to put an unruly bird back in his cage and you can tell a parrot who needs to go to bed "down" as you put the bird in his cage at night.

After your bird has mastered the "up" and "down" commands, encourage him to climb a "ladder" by moving him from index finger to index finger (the "rungs"). Keep taming sessions short (about ten minutes is the maximum conure attention span) and make it fun so taming is enjoyable for both of you.

Petting

After your bird has become comfortable sitting on your hand, try petting him. Birds seem to like to have their heads, backs, cheek patches, under wing areas, and eye areas (including the closed eyelids) scratched or petted lightly. Quite a few like to have a spot low on their back at the base of their tail (over their preen glands) rubbed. Many birds do not enjoy having their stomachs scratched, although yours may think this is heaven!

You'll have to experiment to see where your bird likes to be petted. You'll know you're successful if your bird clicks or grinds his beak, pins his eyes, or settles onto your hand or your lap with a completely relaxed, blissful expression on his face.

Some people may try to tell you that you need to wear gloves while taming your conure to protect yourself from a bite. I recommend against this. A conure generally doesn't bite that hard and wearing gloves will only make your hands appear scarier to your bird. If your pet is scared, taming him will take more time and patience on your part, which may make the process less enjoyable for you both.

Toilet Training

Although some people don't believe it, conures and other parrots can be toilet trained so they don't eliminate on their owners. If you want to toilet train your bird, you will have to choose a word or phrase that will mean the act of eliminating to your pet, such as "poop" or "go potty." While you're training your pet to associate the word or phrase with the action, you will have to train yourself to recognize what body language and actions indicate your conure is about to eliminate, such as shifting around or squatting slightly. Use the phrase every time you see your conure eliminate.

When your bird seems to associate "go potty" with eliminating, you can try picking him up and holding him until he starts to shift or squat. Tell the bird to "go potty" while placing him in his cage, where he can eliminate. When he's done, pick your bird up again and praise him for being such a smart bird!

Expect a few accidents while you are both learning this trick, but soon you'll have a toilet-trained bird. You can put him in his cage about every twenty minutes or so, give him the command, and expect the bird to eliminate on command.

Toilet training will certainly make it a lot more pleasant to have your conure out and about.

Naughty Conures

Training a conure (or any bird) takes lots of time and patience. You must first gain your pet's trust, and then you must ensure you never lose it. To accomplish this, you must be careful not to lose your temper with your bird and never hit him. Birds are very sensitive, intelligent creatures who do not deserve to be hit, no matter how you may feel in a moment of anger.

Although parrots are clever creatures, they are not linear cause-and-effect thinkers. If a parrot commits action A (chewing on some molding under your kitchen cabinets, for example), he won't associate reaction B (you yelling at him, locking him in his cage, or otherwise punishing him) with the misbehavior. As a result, most traditional forms of discipline are ineffective with parrots.

So what do you do when your conure misbehaves? Try to catch him in the act. Look at your bird sternly and tell him "no" in a firm voice. If the bird is climbing or chewing on something, he shouldn't, remove him from the source of danger and temptation as you tell him "no." If your bird has found himself up into a screaming banshee, sometimes a short time out in his cage with the cover on (between five and ten minutes will do in most cases) will do wonders to calm him down. Once the screaming stops and the bird has calmed down enough to play quietly, eat, or simply move around his cage, take the cover off to reveal a well-behaved, calm pet.

Talking Birds

One of the most appealing aspects of conure ownership is this species' reputation as talented talkers. Although many conures learn to talk, none of them are guaranteed to talk. The tips here will help you teach your conure to talk, but please don't be disappointed if your bird never utters a word.

Remember that language, whether it's conure or human, helps members of a species or group communicate. Most baby birds learn the language of their parents because it helps them communicate with their family and their flock. A pet conure raised with people may learn to imitate the sounds he hears his human family make, but if you have more than one conure, the birds may find communicating with each other easier and more enjoyable than trying to learn your language.

Most experts say that the best time to teach a conure to talk is between the time he leaves the nest and his first birthday. If you have an adult conure, the chances of him learning to talk are lower than if you start with a young bird. Male birds may be more likely to talk, but I have heard of some talkative females, too.

Talking Training Tips

You will be more successful in training a conure to talk if you keep a single pet bird, rather than a pair. Birds kept in pairs or groups are more likely to bond with other birds than with people. By the same token, don't give your bird any toys with mirrors on them if you want the bird to learn to talk since your bird will think the bird in the mirror is a potential cagemate with whom he can bond.

Start with a young bird, because the younger the bird is, the more likely he is to want to mimic human speech. Pick one phrase to start with. Keep it short and simple, such as the bird's name.

Say the phrase slowly, so the bird learns it clearly. Some people teach their conures to talk by rattling off words and phrases quickly, only to be disappointed when the bird repeats them in a blurred jumble that cannot be understood.

Be sure to say the chosen phrase with emphasis and enthusiasm. Birds like drama and seem to learn words that are said emphatically—which may be why some of them pick up the bad language so quickly!

Try to use phrases that make sense in context. For instance, say "good morning" or "hello" when you uncover the bird's cage each day. Say "goodbye" when you leave the room, or ask "want a treat?" when you offer your conure his meals.

Phrases that make sense are also more likely to be used by you and other members of your family when conversing with your bird. The more your bird hears an interesting word or phrase, the more likely he is to say that phrase some day.

Don't change the phrase around. If you're teaching your bird to say "hello," for example, don't say "hello" one day, then "hi" the next, followed by "hi, Petey!" (or whatever your bird's name is) another day.

Keep training sessions short. Conure breeders recommend ten-to fifteen-minute sessions.

Train your bird in a quiet area. Think of how distracting it is when someone is trying to talk to you with a radio or a television blaring in the background. It's hard to hear what the other person is saying under those conditions, isn't it? Your conure won't be able to hear you any better or understand what you are trying to accomplish if you try to train him in the midst of noisy distractions. Be sure to keep your conure involved in your family's routine, though, because isolating him completely won't help him feel comfortable and part of the family. Remember that a bird needs to feel comfortable in his environment before he will draw attention to himself by talking.

What a Companion conure Expects

Tolerance
Only the most tolerant of people will be able to coexist with a conure, especially a medium to large bird. Not only is there noise and mess, but there's also the occasional bite, mischief to handle, and fussiness to contend with. And you have to take it all in your stride.

Empathy
Realize that a conure isn't meant to live in a home, though he can be quite happy if cared for properly. Don't get angry if your bird is demanding. He's just acting like a bird. Try to empathize. Imagine what it's like to be that conure. Is he locked in a cage a lot of the day? Does he have the right things to eat? Does he have enough to play with? Try to look at life through his eyes.

Sense of humor
If you can't laugh, you'll end up crying. Conures do all kinds of chaotic things, such as chew the piano legs, make holes in walls, and poop on your taxes. Turn your back for an instant, and you never know what your bird is getting into. But remember, it's not your bird's fault. It's yours. So laugh at the things your bird does. Parrots can be quite humbling.

Attentiveness
An attentive conure guardian knows his or her bird so well, and it's obvious when there are any changes, either physical and behavioral. Once these signs become readily visible, and it may be too late to help the bird. However, if you know your bird well, you'll know all of his little nuances.

Decisiveness and action

If you do happen to run into a birdy emergency, or you believe your bird is ill, you can't sit around and wait for things to get better. A conure needs a decisive guardian who will rush to the veterinarian when necessary.

Constant companionship

Conures aren't fond of being alone and won't stand for neglect very long. Behavioral problems result from loneliness, as do physical issues. If you have a lone bird or even a few conures that all consider you their main squeeze, you'll have to set aside a considerable amount of time to interact and play.

A loyal friend

Above all, a conure needs you to be a loyal friend who doesn't run at the first signs of trouble. Before you ditch the relationship for whatever reason, do yourself and your conure a favor and consult an expert. Many good bird behaviorists and consultants are available to help you with issues that arise. No need to dump the bird, even if it seems like he might be dumping you. Behavior issues are often temporary or remedied with a simple plan of activities

Encouraging Your Conure to Talk

Be patient with your conure. Stop the sessions if you find you are getting frustrated. Your conure will sense that something is bothering you and will react by becoming bothered himself. This is not an ideal situation for you or your bird. Try to keep your mood upbeat. Smile a lot and praise your pet when he does well! Graduate to more difficult phrases as your bird masters simple words.

Consider keeping a log of the words your bird knows. (This is especially helpful if more than one person will be working with the conure). When you aren't talking to your conure, try listening to him. Conures and other birds sometimes mumble to themselves to practice talking as they drift off to sleep. Because your conure may have a small voice, you'll have to listen carefully to hear whether your pet is making progress.

You're probably wondering whether the talking tapes and CDs sold in pet supply stores and through advertisements in bird magazines work. The most realistic answer I can give is "sometimes." Some birds learn from the repetition of the tapes and CDs that, fortunately, have gotten livelier and more interesting in recent years.

Other birds benefit from having their owners make tapes of the phrases the bird is currently learning and hearing those tapes when their owners aren't around. I recommend against playing a constant barrage of taped phrases during the day because the bird is likely to get bored hearing the same thing for hours on end. If he's bored, the bird will be more likely to tune out the tape and the training.

Finally, if you're patient, consistent training seems to be going nowhere, you may have to accept the fact that your conure isn't going to talk. Don't be too disappointed if your pet doesn't learn to talk. Most birds don't, and talking ability should never be the primary reason for owning a bird. If you end up with a non-talking pet, continue to love him for the unique creature he is.

The Trick to Training Your Conure

One of the best ways to spend time with your conure is to teach him to do simple tricks. Your bird will come to expect and enjoy the extra attention you give him during training sessions, and you will see a stronger bond develop between you and your bird as the training progresses.

Before you begin to teach your conure tricks, make sure you have the patience and perseverance to undertake training sessions. Birds sometimes behave as we expect them to, but sometimes they want to do what they want to do, and it's up to you not to become frustrated or angry with your pet when he does not behave as you expect. Anger and frustration can damage the relationship you have with your bird, so be sure to be patient and cheerful during each training session.

As you begin to plan what tricks you will teach your conure, notice what your bird likes to do and make it part of his trick training. You will soon find it's much easier to expand on one or more of your bird's natural behaviors, and that will make trick training easier and more enjoyable for both of you. For example, some conures like to climb while others enjoy holding their wings in the air and stretching (this can be turned into an eagle pose without too much effort). Still, others amuse themselves by using their beaks to examine a wide variety of items in their environment, and you can teach them to touch objects as you name them.

Trick Training Tips

To make the most of your parrot training sessions, keep the following points in mind:

• Know what your bird likes and dislikes. If your bird is naturally playful, he will be a better candidate to learn tricks than a bird who is content to sit on his owner's hand for head scratching.
• Provide several short training sessions each day. Pet birds have short attention spans, and they tend to become cranky if you try to teach them something once you've exceeded that attention span. Ten minutes or less, several times a day, is usually more effective than one longer session.
• Make the sessions fun. Remember that these training sessions are supposed to be enjoyable for both you and your bird, and immediately end any session that is not going well.
• Reward your bird's good behavior with a combination of food treats, verbal praise, petting, or cuddling. If your bird loves to have his nape scratched, for instance, give this area extra attention when your bird performs his trick correctly. This way he will learn to respond to different types of rewards, rather than just waiting for a favorite food treat to come his way.
• Appreciate your bird for the unique individual he is. Love your bird because he is your pet, not because of the tricks he can do. Some birds are natural show-offs; others are more reserved. If you have a quick trick learner, teach the bird tricks and add to his repertoire over time. If your bird doesn't seem to enjoy learning tricks, don't force it. Appreciate your bird for his other wonderful qualities and love him as your pet.

Tricks to Teach Your Conure

Your conure is a bright bird and can learn to perform a wide variety of tricks. His repertoire of learned behaviors is limited only by your imagination and your patience during the training process. Listed here are some beginning tricks to teach your pet. As your training skills improve, you will undoubtedly come up with some tricks that are unique to you and your bird. Good luck, and remember to have fun!

Ride in a Wagon

A conure who is outgoing and unafraid of new toys or new people is a good candidate to learn to ride in a wagon or even a radio-controlled car. If your bird is shy, though, he may not enjoy riding in a toy vehicle, and you might want to try a different trick instead.

To teach your conure to ride in a wagon, you must first get your bird accustomed to the vehicle. Roll the wagon or drive the car in front of your pet to show him what it will do. Praise the bird if he does not run away from the moving vehicle and reassure him that he will be okay if the vehicle motion seems frightening.

After a few days of short sessions of watching the wagon or car roll by, put your bird in the vehicle. Let him sit in it without moving the wagon. Praise and pet your conure as he sits in the wagon, and continue to get the bird accustomed to the vehicle by letting him sit in it for brief periods over several days.

When your bird seems completely comfortable sitting in the wagon, move it a short distance. Praise your conure for his good behavior if he sits calmly, or comfort and reassure your pet if he seems excited or anxious over the vehicle's movement. Put your bird in the vehicle for short rides several times a day, and gradually increase the length of time spent and distance traveled during the rides.

Nod Your Head

A conure who interacts well with his owner and is unafraid of showing off for strangers is a good candidate to learn to nod his head yes and shake his head no.

To teach your bird to nod his head, hold a small portion of his favorite treat just out of reach of his beak and slowly bob it up and down. Your conure will nod his head as he follows the motion of the treat, trying to catch it with his beak. Give his verbal praise, such as, "Is that a yes?" as he nods, so he will associate the words with the motion.

Practice this trick with the treat and the verbal praise, and gradually increase the praise while eliminating the treat.

To teach your conure to shake his head no, repeat the preceding steps but move the treat side to side instead of up and down, so your bird's head will shake side to side to indicate no. Provide different verbal praise, such as, "Is that a no?" as you move the treat from side to side.

Pose Like an Eagle

A conure who enjoys being petted under his wings is a very good candidate to learn to pose like an eagle. Birds who do not enjoy being petted under their wings can also learn this trick, but training them may take a little longer.

Start your training by gently tickling your conure under each wing tip with your index finger. This will cause your conure to raise his wings. Praise him at this point by saying something like "good eagle, good bird" so your conure will begin to associate the word "eagle" with raising his wings.

Practice the combination of gentle tickling and verbal praise at each training session. Increase the use of verbal praise and decrease the tickling until your conure responds to your words alone.

Play Dead

A conure who enjoys being pet and is willing to be turned over by his owner is a good candidate for learning to play dead. First, you must get your bird accustomed to the feel of your hand on his back as he perches on his cage or play gym. When the bird seems comfortable with your hand on his back, hold him between your hands on his side.

After your conure is used to being held on his side between your hands, move to holding him on his back between your hands. Once he seems content to lie this way, remove the hand you have on your bird's feet or belly, and you have a bird playing dead in your hand!

A friend of mine trained her cockatoo to go to sleep in this way, and he enjoys showing off his trick to her friends. She flips the bird over in her hands, tells him, "night-night," and he responds with a "night-night" of his own. He closes his eyes, and she carries him to his cage, where he climbs onto his sleeping perch for the night. She is the only person in her family the bird allows to do this trick—he doesn't seem to think anyone else can get it right!

Your bird must have an incredible amount of trust in you before he allows you to flip him over onto his back. If your conure seems distressed when you flip him onto his back, teach him another trick instead of causing his undue stress by insisting he learns this one.

Conclusion

Birds' small size makes them good pets for today's smaller living spaces. More individuals are living in apartments, mobile or manufactured homes, or condominiums, which makes it awkward and inconvenient to keep a large pet who needs a yard and lots of regular exercises. Birds just seem to fit better in apartments, condos, mobile homes, and other smaller living spaces.

Birds interact well with their owners. Although a bird isn't as blindly loyal as the average dog, he is far more interactive than a fish, a hamster, or even a guinea pig. As a bonus, many birds can learn to whistle or talk, which is unique among pets and which many bird owners find amusing and entertaining.

Birds require consistent, but not constant, attention. This can be a plus for today's busy single people and families. Although birds can't be ignored all day, they are content to entertain themselves for part of the day while their owners are busy elsewhere.

Copyright and Trademarks: This publication is Copyrighted 2017 by Zoodoo Publishing. All products, publications, software and services mentioned and recommended in this publication are protected by trademarks. In such instance, all trademarks & copyright belong to the respective owners. All rights reserved. No part of this book may be reproduced or transferred in any form or by any means, graphic, electronic, or mechanical, including photocopying, recording, taping, or by any information storage retrieval system, without the written permission of the authors. Pictures used in this book are either royalty free pictures bought from stock-photo websites or have the source mentioned underneath the picture.

Disclaimer and Legal Notice: This product is not legal or medical advice and should not be interpreted in that manner. You need to do your own due-diligence to determine if the content of this product is right for you. The author and the affiliates of this product are not liable for any damages or losses associated with the content in this product. While every attempt has been made to verify the information shared in this publication, neither the author nor the affiliates assume any responsibility for errors, omissions or contrary interpretation of the subject matter herein. Any perceived slights to any specific person(s) or organization(s) are purely unintentional. We have no control over the nature, content and availability of the web sites listed in this book. The inclusion of any web site links does not necessarily imply a recommendation or endorse the views expressed within them. Zoodoo Publishing takes no responsibility for, and will not be liable for, the websites being temporarily unavailable or being removed from the Internet. The accuracy and completeness of information provided herein and opinions stated herein are not guaranteed or warranted to produce any particular results, and the advice and strategies, contained herein may not be suitable for every individual. The author shall not be liable for any loss incurred as a consequence of the use and application, directly or indirectly, of any information presented in this work. This publication is designed to provide information in regards to the subject matter covered. The information included in this book has been compiled to give an overview of the subject s and detail some of the symptoms, treatments etc. that are available to people with this condition. It is not intended to give medical advice. For a firm diagnosis of your condition, and for a treatment plan suitable for you, you should consult your doctor or consultant. The writer of this book and the publisher are not responsible for any damages or negative consequences following any of the treatments or methods highlighted in this book. Website links are for informational purposes and should not be seen as a personal endorsement; the same applies to the products detailed in this book. The reader should also be aware that although the web links included were correct at the time of writing, they may become out of date in the future.

Made in the USA
Las Vegas, NV
08 June 2021

24422462R00056